A Pilot Project

Developing Leisure Identities

Judith McGill

A Project of Brampton Caledon Community Living and the
Ontario Ministry of Citizenship, Culture and Recreation

Published by:
>   Brampton Caledon Community Living
>   34 Church St. W.
>   Brampton, Ontario L6X 1M3
>   Canada

Canadian Cataloging in Publication Data

McGill, Judith, 1959–
>   Developing Leisure Identities: A Pilot Project

Includes bibliographical references.
ISBN 0-9680934-0-X

1. Handicapped – Recreation. 2. Handicapped –
Psychology. 3. Leisure – Psychological aspects.
4. Identity (Psychology).   I. Brampton Caledon
Community Living (Organizations).   II. Title.

GV183.5.M34   1996   790.1'96   C96-931652-6

ISBN number: 0-9680934-0-X

This project was financially assisted by the Ontario Ministry of Citizenship, Culture and Recreation

Cover Illustration: Teachers in Training at the Rudolf Steiner Institute,
>   Toronto, Ontario, Canada

Typesetting and Design: Becker Associates

Printed in Toronto, Canada

Dedication

This book is dedicated to Ryan Wilkieson
and his mother, whose untimely deaths
taught me a lot about life.

Table of Contents

List of Figures

Preface

Brampton Caledon Community Living is an Association that supports people with intellectual disabilities in all areas of everyday life. It provides support to families, places for people to live, support for people to gain work in the community, to go to regular schools and to be part of their communities through leisure pursuits.

Three years ago, a core group of people within the Association began to develop a vision for providing support in the area of leisure that would go beyond signing people up for recreation programs through the local municipal recreation department, having people participate in segregated bowling leagues and operating their own "in house" sports leagues. This group, which developed into a Leisure Committee, set as its primary goal to support individuals to develop, strengthen and/or maintain strong leisure roles and related identities.

The Leisure Committee entered into a joint demonstration project with the Ontario Ministry of Citizenship, Culture and Recreation over a one and a half year period. Initially, the project supported eleven adults who were living either semi-independently or at home with their parents. In the final stages of the project, the support was extended to include adults living in "home sharing" arrangements with unrelated adults, and children and teens still living with their families. For the first year of the project there were four part-time leisure support workers hired to provide intense, direct support to individuals. During the final stages, one part-time staff was left to document the project and provide support to individuals and families. The project's goals are set out in Table One on the next page.

Now, more than ever, it is critical to understand how supporting people with disabilities to gain access to valued leisure roles contributes to their building strong ties to their community. The process of supporting the development and/or maintenance of leisure identities is a process of dramatically changing how individuals with disabilities think about themselves, and how these individuals are defined by others. This resource book provides a starting place for exploring a radically new orientation to leisure support and leisure services.

Table One
Project Goals

Primary Goals

- To help the people included in the project be active, valued members of their communities with valued social roles.
- To help the people included in the project develop, strengthen or maintain strong leisure roles and related identities.
- To assist the people included in the project to strengthen their sense of belonging to the community through building connections and relationships in the "associational sector," e.g., leisure clubs, associations and groups.
- To document the stories of the individuals who are in the project so that their experiences can be shared with other communities and provide important learnings.

Support-Related Goals

- To help the people included in the project go after their dreams, and feel safe expressing their dreams and passions.
- To help the people included in the project develop the will to pursue their leisure passions.
- To assist the people included in the project go beyond viewing leisure as diversionary, sporadic activities and to find out what lights them up and creates a drive to discover life.
- To assist the people included in the project and their families, expand their definition of leisure roles beyond stereotypical notions including sports figures and movie stars.
- To assist families to become more aware and supportive of their son's and/or daughter's leisure passions.
- To introduce the people included in the project to others in the community who have similar passions and to continue to support those relationships.
- To help the people included in the project articulate and express their needs in a variety of ways so that support persons can take direction from them.
- To learn how to take direction from and be guided by the individuals included in the project.
- To assist the people included in the project hold a vision of themselves as strong, active members of their communities.

Acknowledgments

Special thanks go to my friends Sue Reid-Kulpaka and Gloria Christianson who not only gave me encouragement, but who always provided a warm, supportive ear throughout the process.

I would like to acknowledge the contributions of Donna Arsenault, Dejan Obradovic, and Elias Tabar, leisure support workers in Brampton, for their commitment to pioneering these concepts and approaches. I consider them co-creators of this process. I would equally like to thank the members of Brampton Caledon Community Living's Leisure Committee for their enthusiastic support: James Cregg, Chris Cregg, Rick Martin, Angela Williams-Critchlow, Ahmed Iqbal, Sharon Bonnello, John Kearns, Lucy Russo, Mike McAstocker and Margerite Reed. I would also like to acknowledge Jack Kelly, whose writing in the area of leisure identities not only inspired me but also gave me the confidence to pursue my own insights.

I feel I have been privileged to come to know the families and individuals that have been part of this project. All of them have taught me a lot about leisure identities and for that I am deeply thankful.

I am grateful to Joe Cawthorpe for his unwavering support for this work and for allowing me the space I needed to innovate.

I would like to thank the following individuals who assisted me by reviewing copies of the manuscript and acting as my mirrors to the outer world: Diane Myers, Pat Anthony, Sharon Bonnello, Heather Burns, Pauline Steinmann, Pam Tuff, Jim Cregg, Cindy Bobinski, Connie Melanson-Savoy, Joe Cawthorpe, David Jory, Sara Burnett-Smith, Linda Sereda, Pam Lillos, Martin Carriere, Terry Alyman, Carrie Schell, Miles Schell, Felicia Jervis, Sue Reid-Kulpaka, Gloria Christianson and Margerite Reed. I am also especially grateful to Lindsay Morgan for her superb editorial work on the book.

This project and this book would not have been possible without the financial support of the Ontario Ministry of Citizenship, Culture and Recreation. Thanks to David McCrindle, Herb Gray and Jerry Dupas who provided the Ministry support.

Finally, writing for days on end would not be possible if it weren't for the gracious support of my husband Doug Wylie and my children Meredith and Rebecca! Thanks go to them for supporting me to follow my passions.

Introduction

There are a few main realms in our lives in which we carve out certain roles for ourselves and derive our sense of who we are. These are the areas of work and school, family and intimate groups, society at large, community and leisure. Life provides an opportunity to explore a multitude of different roles within these realms. It is this "trying on" of different roles that gives our lives excitement and relieves the boredom. It is this experimentation that forces our definitions of ourselves to stay fluid and in constant flux. We can be at once mother, writer, dancer, workshop organizer, aunt and friend. Each role overlaps and influences all the others as it shifts and changes. We spend our lives integrating the many different roles into a coherent whole.

I am not who I was yesterday nor who I will be tomorrow.

When new roles are embraced, old ones can be discarded or allowed to lie dormant, to be taken up at some other time. Roles can be established that complement or even challenge existing ones. Still other roles endure over time and provide a consistent backdrop from which to experiment. Consider Sarah:

> Sarah can't wait for spring to be here. She is a gardener. Spring is when she feels the most alive. Spring is when she feels she has been reawakened and brought out of the cold dark sleep of winter. When you talk to Sarah in the winter, she will describe it in various shades of grey. She experiences winter as if she had entered into a period of hibernation or dormancy, much like the seeds and geraniums she guards in her basement. Her passion's flame is kept alive by poring over seed and bulb catalogues and dreaming about this year's garden. She longs to immerse herself in the smell and feel of damp, fresh earth.

> As buds come on the trees, and she sees evidence of life, she is filled with a beaming radiance. She is full of hope all over again. She begins talking about her plans for this year's garden. She is bursting with enthusiasm and anticipation. She goes into minute details about the new species she plans to introduce to this or that section of the garden. She shows you the intricate plot plans she has drawn in pastels that enable her to begin to visualize the interplay of colours she expects to create. Her expressions are full of bright colours and images. She begins searching out expert gardeners to get advice about the suitability of this species over another and this product versus another.

As soon as she can, she dons her magenta-coloured apron and wide-brimmed hat and begins labouring over the garden plots. She takes time thinning out plants that have gotten out of hand, pulling weeds, spreading mulch, watering the tender shoots and cultivating the soil. She spends hours with her children, helping them prepare a tiny garden plot for them to nurture and fuss over. As the garden begins to take shape, she basks in the sense of accomplishment it gives her. She marvels at how her gardens are able to reflect something of her moods.

Her passion wakes her up to other things as well. She now finds time to be out in her yard and more present in her neighbourhood. She usually spends her mornings out and about in her garden, chatting with friendly passersby and neighbours who wonder what this year's garden will bring. In the afternoon she goes for long neighbourhood walks, taking in the fragrances and vivid colours of flowers and vegetation. She steps out of her inner reflectiveness. She begins getting out more and attending lectures at the Royal Botanical Gardens on growing certain rose varieties. She also starts catching up with friends she has met over the years who also enjoy gardening. When her sister visits, she digs up some Iris rhizomes to give her for her garden. She takes the opportunity to pass on some of her expertise.

In late summer she organizes the annual flower show at her church. She acts as a judge in the hybrid rose category. Last year her sister entered the contest and won honourable mention. It gives Sarah great pleasure to know that it was her own passion for gardening that inspired her sister to take it up. Sarah considers her experience and knowledge in gardening a gift that she has to offer others. She is always willing to share it with others.

Sarah hasn't always been a gardener. She took it up once her children started school. She began with a small vegetable garden in the side yard. Initially, she found it was a way to get her outside in the summer and help her get to know her neighbours. Having very young children had been an isolating experience for Sarah. Gardening balanced her family obligations with something she could do for herself while the children played.

Taking up gardening gave her a sense of being connected to her past. She had been raised on a farm near Sydney, Nova Scotia. She can remember spending hours watching her grandmother tend her rose garden and herb garden. Seeing the care and reverence her grand-mother had for plants left a powerful impression on Sarah. She fondly recalls the sweet smells she enjoyed, as she played tag with her sisters among the long rows of roses. Each plant was carefully staked and named. She remembers the times that she and her siblings would play a memory game and try to be the first to remember the name of each rose plant. Her grandmother had lovingly named one of her yellow hybrid roses after her, using her nick name, Sarah Lou. All of these cherished memories flood back in some way each time Sarah takes up her hoe and begins working the earth around her tender plants.

Sarah's leisure identity has grown over time. As a child, she was exposed to gardening by watching her grandmother toil in the gardens. The interest lay dormant in her until there was a space in her life to take it up. The smells, the pleasures, all lay there waiting to be reactivated. She may have been spurred on by a desire to reminisce about her childhood as she herself was struggling to deal with early motherhood. Or maybe she just felt the need to take up an interest that would get her out into the yard and meet the neighbours. Her passion is forever growing and changing and exposing her to ever more opportunities in all aspects of her life. Even though many of the roles we adopt remain with us over time, this does not mean they are static. A mother of an infant takes on a far different role than the mother of a teenager. As role demands and expectations change, so too do our commitments to the role. We commit to a particular role by devoting time, energy and money to it, or divest ourselves of a role by spending less and less time, energy and money on it. The importance of each role to our self-valuation can be witnessed by the relative investments and or commitments we make to it. As our commitment to the role begins to increase, so too does our interest in competency development and mastery. We are motivated to learn the skills necessary to "take on the role." The more competent we feel in a role, the more likely we are to further develop it into an identity and begin to refer to ourselves by that identity, e.g., "I am an organic gardener."

Each culture defines to some extent what the acceptable or typical expectations are for any given role. Once we have begun to commit ourselves to a particular role, we are much more interested in where the boundaries of conformity and non-conformity exist, or in other words, how much we can experiment with the role within the usual parameters generally given.

Each person's unique interpretation of the role is what is called the "identity." The identity best describes who you are and what you are striving for within the boundaries of a particular role. It is through "trying on" various aspects of a given role and feeling comfortable with the expectations of it, that we begin to individualize or interpret it for ourselves.

All the world's a stage,
and all the men and women
*   merely players.*

They have their exits and their
*   entrances;*
And one man in his time
*   plays many parts...*

Shakespeare: *As You Like It*

Once we become involved in exploring the many aspects of gardening, for instance, we are making an initial commitment to the role of "gardener." If we enjoy the role and find it satisfying, this commitment often deepens over time. We discover ourselves wanting to learn as much as we can about gardening, and wanting to spend more and more time at it. We talk to others about it. We gradually begin to develop skills and expand our knowledge of gardening (e.g., what to plant, when to plant). As a result, we begin to know more about what aspects of gardening we like and don't like and begin developing our preferences. Once we broaden our understanding of the role, we can then define which aspects we most want to identify with and take for ourselves. This identification with the role contributes to building the identity.

As the identity emerges our self-perception begins to change. We begin to see ourselves as "a gardener" and want to differentiate our interests from those of other gardeners. We begin to describe ourselves to others in a particular way. "I am an organic vegetable gardener. I am really not interested in perennial gardening." This assists others in formulating a clear view of what our interests are and where our passions lie. It is through this process of defining and redefining our interests and interpreting them to others that they are able to develop a more vivid picture of who we are. This picture of who we are, what our talents are, and what we get passionate about, contributes to the way in which we become known in our communities, among our neighbours, our families and friends. Over time, our reputations are built in this way.

Very often, we begin exploring a particular role only to find that it is something we don't enjoy, or that it doesn't seem to fit with who we are and what we are good at. When this happens, we have a choice either to abandon the activity altogether or to continue doing it on an occasional basis. By making a short term investment of time, energy and money, and taking the opportunity to explore the role, we have been able to rule it out as something we want to pursue. This process of investing and divesting in various roles is part of the natural rhythm of developing a coherent "self."

The process of "taking on an identity" is a long and gradual one. The identity begins to emerge over time as commitments are made and as the passion evolves. When we have really chosen something that we are passionate about, an initial interest blossoms into a lifelong pursuit.

> *Leisure is able to provide a unique context for learning about who we are and who we might become. Taking time for leisure can be the time that we take to discover ourselves and our passions.*

Many of us take our leisure identities for granted. We rarely reflect on how an occasional leisure interest blossomed into something that has begun to define who we are and how we describe ourselves. We seldom take time to think about how an activity we used to participate in occasionally began to develop into a passion, and to take up a huge portion of our time, energy and money. We take for granted the gradual process of seeing ourselves and having others see us more and more as a "gardener," a "golfer" or a "photographer," for example. We are often unconscious of what being a "gardener" means to us, what purpose it plays in our lives, how it has altered our relationships and our self image. These aspects of the role are likely to stay unconscious unless for some reason they are threatened and we need to become conscious of why they are important in our lives.

It is important to make a conscious study of the shift that takes place in leisure when people go beyond just participating in an activity and actually begin to pursue the leisure role over time and develop it into a leisure identity. By bringing consciousness to the way in which we develop our leisure interests into leisure identities we:

- gain an understanding of the multiple ways in which we are either supported or not supported by others to express, develop and maintain our leisure identities;
- come to realize how we have or have not succeeded in safeguarding or making room for our leisure "passions" amongst other competing roles and identities in our lives like work and family;
- learn more about what gives us meaning and pleasure, and what we hold to be most important in life;
- understand more fully how we each create either balance or imbalance in our lives between our work, family, community and leisure roles;
- see more clearly how each of our roles overlap and weave to create the complex whole that we have become, and how each role either complements or contrasts with the others.

Becoming more conscious of how we use the time available to us for leisure means considering the balance between our commitment to ourselves and to our work, family and community obligations.

Leisure serves a number of purposes in our lives at any one time. It can be a rich soil from which to derive a sense of who we are, and to discover what we like and what our individual gifts are. It can also be a vehicle for escaping our routine or for finding enjoyment in life. As well, it can serve as a context for developing and strengthening relationships. We each tend to approach our leisure experiences differently depending on what we are hoping to get out of them.

If we are searching to balance out our work and family identities, leisure can be an attractive realm to explore another dimension of ourselves. Many of us are attracted to developing or strengthening a leisure identity as a way of going beyond those involvements that have come to symbolize our obligations, duties and commitments to others. We are searching for something that we can do voluntarily for ourselves, in a realm where we are accountable only to ourselves and where our investments, intensity and interest can fluctuate with our own rhythms and passion. When work and family identities overpower us and begin taking over our life, leisure identities can offer balance.

At times when we feel we are just needing a break, our leisure involvement will be much different. It is at these times that we focus on finding an experience that will be novel and stimulating, that will allow us to escape or balance our everyday existence, that will get us out of our familiar settings, and/or that will allow us to leave our troubles behind. It is not so important what we do, but just that we do something. This kind of leisure experience can be referred to as "diversionary/escapist," "thrill-seeking," "rejuvenating" or "event oriented" leisure. Because there is not a lot of emphasis placed on which activity is undertaken, there is very little expectation that the activity will come to define who we are. The pattern of involvement is usually sporadic and uneven, and for this reason does not necessarily lead to developing particular competencies.

There are many other times when we seek out leisure experiences for the purpose of being with another person, or within a group. In this instance, the relationship is paramount and the activity secondary. The desire is to find an activity that will bring you together either with one other person or a group of people.

Leisure Identities and Persons with Disabilities:

Our culture devalues persons with disabilities. As a result, they are less likely to have access to the valued social roles that most of us take for granted. In fact, society unconsciously casts persons with disabilities into negatively valued roles like dependent person, object of charity, holy innocent, eternal child, object of ridicule and pity, menace or object of dread. (Wolfensberger, 1983). These negatively valued roles are perpetuated to the extent that members of society rarely question them. As a society, we come to expect persons with disabilities to be in dependent roles. We have learned to severely limit our role expectations for persons with disabilities. The impact of these lowered expectations can be devastating. One of the most damaging effects is the likelihood that persons with disabilities will internalize these lowered expectations. By internalizing these negative roles and negative expectations, the individual creates a self-fulfilling prophecy. In other words, "I become what you think I am."

As a result of being cast into negative roles and having limited access to valued social roles, people with disabilities very often become dependent on "human services" and others for their survival. This dependency on human services creates significant discontinuities in their lives, especially in the area of relationships. Support staff often come and go in their lives. This constant shifting of relationships and support leads to enormous insecurity on the part of the person with a disability. Physical and social isolation further contributes to the problem.

As a consequence of these discontinuities, people with disabilities typically end up putting an inordinate amount of time and energy into their so-called "survival needs." That is, worrying about where they will live, what they will do and who will be there for them.

Leisure is rarely recognized as a "survival need" in our culture. The unstated argument seems to be that we can survive without being happy or having fun. Other needs take precedence. Once these so-called lower needs are satisfied, then our leisure needs will be considered. It is likely that leisure takes a back seat in our culture because it is so closely linked to pleasure and enjoyment. Pleasure and enjoyment do not seem to fit into a culture that boasts such a strongly embedded work ethic. And yet, each of us still has a deeply-felt sense of our leisure as being essential to our "ability to carry on". We are confronted with the contradiction that while we don't value it, leisure is often what has made life bearable, what has helped us to sort out our priorities, and what has helped to relieve the tensions in our lives, and to build and maintain relationships. Through our leisure involvements we have gained a stronger sense of who we are and have strengthened our sense of belonging.

As a culture, we must begin to recognize the essential connections between humour and performance, play and learning, pleasure and rejuvenation, leisure and relationship-building and finally, leisure and self-actualization. In our culture, *leisure is a survival need.*

The process of marginalization or devaluation has meant that persons with disabilities have been taught to view leisure primarily as a "treat," as a programmed diversion forming part of the monotony of being a client of human services. Leisure as defined in human service terms, has not been recognized as a realm in which people with disabilities can explore or discover who they are and who they might become. There has been little recognition that supporting and allowing people with disabilities to experience the full range of leisure expressions is important to their finding meaning and creating balance in their lives.

For the most part, leisure professionals, human service staff and even family members have been concerned with "keeping individuals occupied" in their leisure by taking them to this or that event, or by signing them up for recreational programs where they can try this or that activity. This is partly, because many of us have not believed that individuals would ever be able to develop the competencies needed to become confident in their leisure. It is also, in part, because we have not until recently had any conceptual framework for understanding and reflecting on the gradual way in which each of us develops a preference for a certain leisure role and then begin individualizing it into an identity. Very little time has been spent holding strong expectations for individuals to express themselves through a particular leisure role. As well, support mechanisms have not yet been developed to provide enough intentional support for individuals to explore their passions fully, and develop strong identities.

As a result of these low expectations, many people with disabilities, have been perpetually kept at the initial stages of leisure identity development. They have been stuck in the "exploration phase" for their entire lives. This "perpetual sampling" is mirrored in the area of work for persons with disabilities. People are expected to stay on work placement for the rest of their lives, to continue to try different job settings without ever making a choice about what they really want to do, which job they prefer most and where their talents lie. There are very few parallels to this predicament in "real life."

Leisure Identities: Thinking it Through

Developing Leisure Identities and Following Our Passions

Passion is defined by *Webster New Collegiate Dictionary* as "a strong liking for or devotion to some activity, object or concept; intense driving e.g. driven to..." Our passion is what compels us to pursue and devote ourselves to certain goals and activities and is one of the strongest expressions of our desires. Desire is defined as "our conscious impulses toward an object or experience that promises enjoyment or satisfaction in its attainment, a longing or craving." Desire then, is what we typically refer to as our wishes.

Most conscious dreaming processes are the unearthing of our true passions and desires. Our passions are intimately connected to our sense of hope. If we can talk freely about our passion or what fires us up, we have a renewed sense of possibility. When we can wish for ourselves, we can reawaken to ourselves.

> *And when a man lives multi-dimensionally, explores all possibilities available, never shrinks back from any challenge, goes, rushes to it, welcomes it, rises to the occasion, then life becomes a flame, life blooms.*
>
> Bhagwan Shree Rajneesh
> *The Sacred Yes*

Our passions are an expression of us. They are connected to our sense of who we are, what we believe in and what we stand for. They help us to better express ourselves and discover ourselves in a variety of realms including relationships, work, leisure and community. They are what make us truly unique, in that very few people have the same constellation of passions. They are what help us to respect our true selves and to come to know who we are.

When you are inspired by some
great purpose, some extraordinary project,
all your thoughts break their bonds.
Your mind transcends limitations,
Your consciousness expands in every direction
and you find yourself in a new, great and
wonderful world.

Dormant forces, faculties and talents
become alive, and you discover yourself
to be a greater person by far
than you ever dreamed
yourself to be.

Patanjali

In our culture, the language of passion has been reserved almost solely for describing the erotic. It has come to mean the hunger we all have to be intimately connected to others in physical or sexual ways. As well, our passions are imagined as the driving force behind the "I" running amuck and going out of control. In other words, if one is following one's passions, one is doing so selfishly, at the expense of others. We have thus been taught that following our passions in leisure is somehow unacceptable or indulgent.

As a work-centred society, we have come to measure our worth by what we contribute, what we produce, and ultimately what we consume. Because leisure is viewed as non-productive, it is often considered useless. We have not yet as a culture developed a compelling rationale for making a place for leisure in our lives. We do not yet seem to understand its significance in terms of bringing richness to our lives and expanding who we can become. When we do pursue leisure it is often not in order to create balance in our lives or to expand our personal definitions of ourselves, but it is as a "consumer of leisure." Taking a consumer mindset into our leisure experiences destroys some of the essence of it. If we are merely a consumer of leisure, we miss the many opportunities it provides for being an expression of who we are and what we are passionate about.

There are many forces that draw us away from our passions and force our dreams for ourselves to go underground or lie dormant. So many of us get caught up in survival or work ethics. We postpone the pursuit of our desires and/or our passions in the realm of leisure. We put ourselves into a kind of waiting pattern. We wait until we have enough money to pursue something. We wait for the kids to get just a little bit older, more independent. We wait until we have enough free time, or until the renovations are done, the children go off to university, life slows down, or we retire.

Another large part of this practice of putting our leisure and passions on hold is due to the fact that so many of us believe we don't deserve it. We believe we haven't worked hard enough yet, we shouldn't be going off after our own desires when there is still work to be done, we haven't suffered enough, that our life is not settled enough, in short, that there are more important needs to be looked after. We find ourselves searching for complicated rationales for why it's not the right time to take up something that has always given us, or is likely to give us, great pleasure and fulfillment.

As adults, as we wonder whether we "deserve" to balance our work, community, and/or family responsibilities to find time for leisure, we are inundated by all of the old childhood messages we have internalized about play, such as:

"Once all of your homework is done you can go out and play."

"You're getting too old to play."

"All you ever want to do is play, there are chores to be done."

"You act like life is one big game."

The study of leisure identities and its relationship to passion prompts us to ask the most esoteric of all questions, that is "If not now, when?" To live passionately is to live without holding back, to live in the present and in action. Passion does not suggest sitting back and waiting. To go after one's passions is to experience the fullness of life. It is to experience the ordinariness of life in a way that enlivens and enriches. To live passionately is to say "yes" to life.

> Life is like a wild tiger.
> You can either lie down
> and let it
> Lay its paw on your head
> or sit on its back and ride it.
>
> Ride the Wild Tiger

At certain times in adulthood our work roles dominate our lives and make us feel like we are stuck, that we have become one-dimensional, out of balance. This over-attachment to our work roles happens for a number of reasons, not the least of which is the extent to which employers are coming to expect us to devote ourselves to our work if we want to stay employed. It also has to do with where we derive the most potent rewards. Our work role(s) provide us a means of paying the bills. They can also give us a sense of meaning, and a feeling that we are contributing. The rewards in other realms of our lives may be less tangible and therefore considered less potent and desirable.

However, the stagnation and alienation we often feel in mid-career compels us to begin looking for both meaning and balance in our lives. We are confronted with the task of rediscovering our passions in the area of leisure. We are faced with the need for reawakening the spark in us that once gave us a sense of purpose. We are called to look for something in us that gives us genuine pleasure, a sense of timelessness, or allows a retreat, a stepping back to take a look at the world and our lives. This search is one of courage and discovery.

> *Behold the turtle, who makes progress only*
> *when he sticks his neck out.*
>
> Anonymous

Discovering or rediscovering our true passions or dormant leisure roles and identities can open up a whole new range of possibilities in our lives. It can teach us about ourselves, and it will most certainly assist us to find a happier and healthier balance between work/school, family and community roles.

> *Life is either a daring adventure or nothing.*
>
> Helen Keller

Leisure Roles and Identities

Role identity theory explores the ways in which each of us enacts a variety of social roles in our day-to-day lives. It tries to explain the connection between how others define us and how we come to define ourselves. As social beings, "our means of understanding and communicating what we are and might be are learned from others. Through the life course we are always 'becoming' through interaction with others, learning and relearning who we are." (Kelly 1987,94, 104)

It is through our interaction with others that we begin to develop our self-perception and self-image. We interpret the responses of others to our actions and the way we present ourselves. In Charles Cooley's original work (1902;153), he explains that self-image is built by "imagining how we appear to others, interpreting the judgment of others, and experiencing feelings such as pride or shame" about our performance.

All of our social roles are drawn from our participation in everyday life in several spheres including work and school, family and intimate groups, society at large, community and leisure. Table Two on the next page, outlines the typical role spectrum that so-called ordinary citizens usually take for granted and contrasts them to the roles that are most likely to be available to citizens who are devalued.

The last section described how leisure identities are developed by those of us who are not devalued. For persons who have been devalued by society, access to many of these social roles has been denied or made considerably more difficult. For this reason, in 1983, Wolf Wolfensberger began to write about something he called *social role valorization*. The goal of social role valorization is "the creation, support, and defence of valued social roles and life conditions for people who are at risk of social devaluation" (Wolfensberger and Thomas 1983). In order to support valued roles, we need to work at enhancing a person's "social image" or perceived value in the eyes of others, as well as enhancing that person's competencies (Hutchison and McGill 1992;93).

As can be seen in the Typical Role Spectrum on the preceding page, leisure is only one context for supporting valued roles and identities. There are many others. However, leisure provides a particularly powerful context for identity creation and expression, for the following reasons:

- It is most likely to be for its own sake and for the experience itself.
- It can have elements of both disciplined, goal oriented activity as well as immersion in the moment (Kelly 1987).
- It provides a novel space for experimenting and taking risks. It allows role flexibility, enabling us to "try on" new roles without posing serious consequences to our primary roles, commitments and definitions of who we are.
- Through feeling free to take risks, we learn a tremendous amount about ourselves and are able to assess our performance informally and adjust our roles and self perceptions accordingly (Kelly 1987).
- By being experience-based more than outcome-based like school and work, leisure offers ample opportunities for "self-testing" or trying out new skills and competencies.
- Leisure is "the social space in which primary relationships are developed, expressed and enhanced" (Cheek and Burch 1976). For this reason, it is strongly connected to how we form our values and priorities and has a significant role to play in family and community building.
- Leisure offers a certain openness for intimacy and bonding. Many of the expressive elements of intimacy are available through leisure, including affection, humour, self-disclosure, playfulness and other enriching forms of engagement (Cheek and Burch 1976).
- Leisure provides one of the primary means of developing social identification and membership in groups outside of the family, through leisure clubs, organizations and associations that are part of our communities (Kelly 1987).

Table Two
Typical Role Spectrum

Ordinary Citizens	Citizens Devalued by Society
Work and School	
Student	Student
Co-op Student	Trainee
Part-time Employee	Permanently Unemployable
Full-time Employee	Welfare Dependent
Cashier, Lawyer, Doctor, Teacher's Aide,	Token Employee
Lithographer, Waitress,	Volunteer Employee
Bus driver, Accountant	Cheap Labourer
Naturalist, Receptionist, Nurse, Janitor	Supported Employee
Business Partner	Burden of Charity
	Object of dread
	Object of ridicule
Family and Intimate Groups:	
Wife, Husband, Partner	Single Person
Lover	Asexual Person
Mother, Father	Role largely unavailable or
	typically contested
Son, Daughter	Dependent Family member
Brother, Sister	Dependent Family member
Aunt, Uncle	Dependent Family member
Cousin	Dependent Family member
Godmother, Godfather	Object of Pity
Stepmother, Stepfather	Menace or Object of Dread
Friend	Dependent Friend
Best friend	
Acquaintance	Acquaintance
Society at large and Community	
Citizen, Voter,	Human Service Client
Neighbour, Church Member,	Token Member
Member of Community Club or Association	Object of Charity
Member of Upper Class – Lower Class	
Middle Class	Holy Innocent
Volunteer	Eternal Child
Board Member	Welfare Recipient
Leisure	
Figure Skater, Bingo Player, Horseback Rider,	Someone who may take part in these
Sailor, Camper, Tennis Player, Belly Dancer,	activities but is not likely identified by or
Music Fan, Wine Taster, Quilt Maker, Artist,	supported in the role. May be seen as
Painter, Hiker, Sculptor, Bird Watcher, Board	deficient and needing these activities for
Game Lover, Mall walker, Cyclist, Squash Player	therapy rather than fun and fulfillment.

Excerpted and adapted from *Leisure, Integration and Community*, (Hutchison and McGill 1992,94).

Commitments

Engaging in any social role requires us to make certain commitments. These commitments can take many forms. They can be made in time, effort, energy, will, and money. Developing social roles can also require sacrifices, for instance, we may have to choose one role over another at certain times in our lives.

To develop a work career, we are conscious of the need to acquire the necessary educational minimum and perform to certain acceptable standards; and perhaps become a member of a professional body. We recognize the need to be seen by our superiors to be making the necessary commitments of time and energy and to be sufficiently dedicated. When performing the job we learn which commitments are essential and which come more from our love of the role or our need to be identified with it. For example, if I want to "be" a car mechanic, I need to clearly understand what the role involves, what expectations people hold for the role and what performance standards are acceptable. Once I am a car mechanic, it becomes essential for me to put in the required time, effort and dedication, and invest a considerable amount of money in tools. It is also likely that I will develop particular specialties within my occupational choice (Kaplan, 1979).

We are less conscious of the commitments that we make in our "leisure careers" or involvements, even though they are often very similar. There are certain commitments that we make when we are trying to establish ourselves in the role and others that come later, in order to maintain our attachment to the role. We usually become more attached to the role as we make more commitments to it and it begins to matter how others perceive our performance, as well as how we perceive it. For example, if I am just taking up sewing, I'm interested in learning some of the basic stitches and simple patterns. Once I am able to make a basic outfit, I may want to learn more intricate patterns and specialized stitching. I may also become interested in taking specialty courses in surging or smocking. I may even begin to get interested in designing my own clothes and joining a sewing circle. Eventually I will be conscious of the quality of my workmanship and it will matter to me what others think about it. I may also invest in a better sewing machine with more options and capacities. The more committed I am to becoming a "seamstress or tailor" the more likely I am to spend a lot of time shopping for fabrics and accessories and finding avenues for the expression.

Continuity of Self

As we move from one role context and identity to another we take what we have learned and apply it to the next situation. This does not mean that we are never clear about who we are. There is always a "self" that has continuity throughout all of the various role contexts and remains the same. This self acts in a more or less coherent manner as it carries out its many different or multiple identities (Kelly 1987).

Kelly claims that because it takes so much to sustain these various roles according to external and internal expectations, "most adults are in a continual process of juggling, balancing, integrating, separating and reformulating these role engagements." As a result, there are roles in our lives that are "currently central, roles that are in the process of being left behind, and roles that are on the horizon but not yet entered" (1987, 103).

How Leisure Roles Change and Evolve Throughout Life

It is critical for us to recognize the natural ebbing and flowing of our leisure involvements throughout the course of our lives.

> *The river runs wild against the edges of the river bank*
> *until it recedes again and in its flow*
> *it is constantly rewriting the shoreline.*

Our leisure roles and identities change and evolve as we go through life, as we grow and mature. These changes can be attributed to a variety of things. Some sociologists relate changes in our leisure roles primarily to shifts in family roles and commitments. They delineate the essential tasks and expectations of each stage in the family life cycle as we evolve from child to adult, and inventory the impact it is likely to have on one's leisure (Sheehy, 1995).

Other sociologists (Gordon, Gaitz, & Scott 1976) have focussed on the stages of psycho-social development and how we face certain dilemmas of development at each stage of the life course. Children between the ages of 12 and 15 are viewed as being faced with the dilemma of acceptance vs. achievement. They are said to be drawn to leisure involvements that will help establish themselves as independent from their parents. This age group is fascinated with the "forbidden" especially as it relates to intimacy and sexuality. They also struggle to choose between leisure experiences that are viewed as prestigious, like sports, and expressive activities that allow for some meaning (Kelly 1987,74).

There are many forces that shape us, and therefore our leisure, throughout our lives: our socioeconomic status, our social network; our ethnic/cultural identities; our geography; our community affiliations; our gender; our political and religious identities and our family backgrounds.

Our lives and our leisure are changed as circumstances change in our lives: personal tragedies or crises; new phases of physical and emotional maturity; leaving home to go to school; marriage; as job situations change; as we begin to establish a family; when we move; as our children grow and leave home; as we take on responsibility for elderly parents; when we retire. Some of these circumstances involve the changing dynamics of family and relationships, while others focus on different stages of work and personal development.

For whatever reason, there are periods in our lives when our leisure roles and identities are central to who we are and how we invest our time, energy and resources. At other times our "leisure identities" seem to be dormant or inactive. Other role identities dominate or take over our lives in terms of where we commit our time and energy and what we are able to do.

This is true for college and university students for example. During their school years they become so focussed on academics, intimate relationships, part-time work and career involvements, that little time is left for expanding or enhancing their leisure identities. Instead, time and energy is invested in planning and anticipating major roles in the areas of intimacy and career.

For new parents, the roles of mother and father not only dominate but at first overwhelm us until we are able to make the necessary adjustments to our lifestyles and self-perceptions. Mothers, especially those who stay at home to care for their children, are often left feeling they have forfeited or lost all of the personal identities they had built previously, in exchange for the role of mother. Their leisure identities disappear at first, until they are able to begin the complex task of balancing and trading off one role for another. Leisure identities then slowly reemerge. Old interests are reawakened in the individual, or others are developed that are more consistent and compatible with the new roles and identities. Often, during the early years of family life, many parents find that their personal leisure identities are reformulated to include more family-centred engagements like camping, hiking, going on picnics, or cycling.

There are other times when our leisure roles play a more central role in our lives, for example, during periods of sustained unemployment, retirement and during the "empty nest stage" when dependent children have left home and parents are no longer as busy taking care of others.

Several Aspects of Leisure Roles and Identities

The development of leisure roles and related identities is a long and gradual process. Because of this, it can be discouraging at times. When we become discouraged or feel stuck it can be helpful for us to take the time to reflect on different aspects of the process. Through reflection we can come to realize what meaning our participation has for us. By uncovering the meaning we strengthen our attachment to the role.

The questions offered in this section and throughout the book are intended to assist us in becoming more conscious and reflective about the way in which leisure identities can impact our lives. If you are in a support role to someone, it is useful for you to answer these questions for yourself first, so that you can understand their implications in a more personal way. Once the self reflection is complete, the questions can then assist you in reflecting on the leisure identities of the individual you are supporting.

Exploring our Individuality

Our individuality is inseparable from our personality. Personality is defined by *Webster's New Dictionary* as "the organization of the individual's distinguishing character traits, attitudes, or habits and the totality of an individual's behavioral and emotional tendencies."

As we really get to know someone we discover their personality; what they most love to do and what they spend their time doing in a number of realms; within the family, their work and their leisure. What we are discovering in coming to know someone, is the essence of their individuality.

And as each of us goes through the process of individualizing certain roles into an identity, we experience a little more of ourselves, what we like and dislike, what got us to this point in our lives, what makes us serene and content, what makes us feel accomplished, what gives us a sense of balance and what distinguishes us from others.

The process of differentiating ourselves from others and truly discovering which identities best describe who we are, is similar to the path taken by a musician.

> A musician plays a number of instruments and a multitude of melodies before she settles on one instrument to make her own. Then as the devotion for that instrument grows she works and works at tuning it and refining her sound. Only then does she begin to really play the instrument and compose melodies with that instrument that speak about what is in her heart and where her life has taken her.

Some Questions for Reflecting:

How does the leisure identity express your tastes?

What meaning does your participation hold for you?

What kinds of beliefs and values are associated with it?
What impact does it have on the choices you make about life, where you live, lifestyle?...

What has this identity taught you about yourself?

Does where you live influence the identities you have chosen? (For example, as a result of living near the mountains you took up ice climbing).

Do you collect objects and things that are associated with your leisure identity? Are these objects sentimental or functional in relation to the particular identity? For example, race track fans collecting lucky racing programs and leather workers collecting patterns for various styles of purses, and briefcases...

How important is this identity to how you have come to describe yourself?

Has your ethnic/cultural/religious background influenced or contributed to your leisure identity?

What impact has this identity had on your habits?

Relationships

Some leisure identities are of an overtly social nature and the relationship connections are obvious, while others are more solitary. It is helpful to become conscious of the relationship aspect of the leisure identity so that when necessary, intentional supports to an individual can include some form of relationship building.

If you are a baseball player, you are part of a team. Playing baseball is a social activity that requires a lot of interaction, cooperation and interdependence. It involves a fairly intense and rigorous schedule of practices, games and sometimes even social events. The investments in terms of time and energy are quite intense and involve showing commitment to the team. Although baseball is seasonal in nature, there are often ways to stay connected to team members throughout the year. Some teams stay connected by holding informal social get togethers; organizing pro-baseball pools or other kinds of tournaments like slow pitch snow ball, bowling or floor hockey. A large part of being a baseball player may be following the pro and semi-pro leagues either live or on television. This interest in not only playing baseball but also watching baseball can form a cohesive bond between members of a team. Many baseball fans come together to watch the games and share the excitement. Being up to date on the latest pro scores gives people a common experience to relate to and talk about.

On the other hand, if you collect comic books the relationship implications are very different. People who collect things are often attracted to the solitary nature of the identity. They seem satisfied collecting their treasures alone or with one or two chosen friends or family members. People who collect things often have a deep appreciation for what they collect. They want to know as much as they can about the history of the objects, where they were produced or grown and what they were or are used for. They take pleasure when friends express appreciation for their collection and make comments on it; how beautiful it is; how complete; how well recorded; how authentic; how valuable; how varied it is; how much patience it must have taken to find a certain piece for the collection. Collecting involves a lot of sleuthing around and finding people and resources that can help locate certain items. In terms of relationships, while it usually does not have much of an impact on expanding their intimate relationships, it may expand their network of acquaintances. Collectors browse in certain stores; attend trade or swap shows, auctions and conventions; and develop informal networks of like-minded collectors. In terms of investments of time, money and energy, collecting identities can be quite intense.

Some Questions for Reflecting

What does the leisure identity mean in terms of relationships, who you hang around with, who you have come to know?

Does the leisure identity link you into any particular social networks?

Does the leisure identity mean that you belong formally or informally to any groups or clubs? Are there any that you would be interested in joining?

What other kinds of experiences has the leisure identity opened up to you (both related and unrelated)?

How has the leisure identity helped you to develop a reputation in your neighbourhood, workplace, community, among family and friends?

What impact do your investments/commitments in the leisure identity have on you and your family? e.g. time away from them, you being able to teach them something, money spent, how you organize time commitments.

What kinds of leisure identities are you most drawn to – social or solitary pursuits?

Image

Each leisure identity has its own image attached to it. According to Gregory Stone (1962), we "use all the symbols of appearance to announce to others who we are and how we would like to be defined." Clothing is the most obvious way to communicate a particular image. Through dress we try to communicate certain things about who we are and to specify the group we belong to. For instance, if I am to look the part of a "weekend hiker" I am likely to wear lightweight hiking boots, a Tilley hat and carry a day pack. "Mountain hikers" however, look different. They are apt to invest in and wear goretex gaiters and jackets, full shank hiking boots and a sturdy hat, and tie an airhorn to their backpack. Some of these aspects of image are closely tied to fashion while others are more tied to style and function.

Some aspects of image are subtle while others are not so subtle. More subtly attached to image are other aspects of the clothing e.g. hikers dress in layers so that they can adapt to the changes in weather on the trail by adding or removing a layer if needed. Weekend casual hikers may layer with t-shirts and sweaters while more serious mountain hikers layer with survival clothing made with goretex, fleece and spun polyester, designed to minimize dampness and keep in heat.

Many of us have had an experience at some time in our lives of trying out a particular leisure interest without being properly outfitted. Through these experiences of not fitting in, it becomes painfully clear to us how essential it is to pay attention to "image" as well as function. For example, you may remember how embarrasing it was to be on the ski hill learning to ski wearing blue jeans and a winter jacket, freezing your legs, while everyone else was in the more appropriate ski-wear.

> *Clothing is only an initial symbol of our identity...it is reinforced by demeanour, posture, vocabulary and manner of speaking and a series of other signs and symbols.*

(Kelly 100)

We also strive to differentiate ourselves by the way we use "identity-specific" language. This language acts as a form of jargon or coded language that signals to others that we belong. The more we begin to invest in a particular identity the more we are likely to learn and be initiated into its language. The slang, the phrases and idiosyncratic terms, are commonly used as a way of creating a sense of solidarity among members of a particular group as well as making communication more efficient and effective. Some of the terms and language have a certain function while others have more to do with image and belonging. In yacht racing for example, terms like beating, hard to the wind, close reach, upward leg, broaching, and clocking are commonly used. Black Jack Players use terms like going bust, double, hit me, stand, and ante up.

Over and over again, leisure support workers in the project have observed, how much "looking the part" contributes to "learning the part." They have seen how important it is for persons who are devalued to "speak the language" and to get to know the customs of a particular leisure interest, in order to feel a sense of belonging, and send the message that they belong. Image specific clothing, language, gestures and ritual are all subtle aspects of membership and belonging. They act as a means for establishing contact and forming an identification with others (Wolfensberger 1983).

Some Questions for Reflecting:

Does this leisure identity have a certain look? e.g. specialized clothing, grooming, gestures...

What kinds of possessions/equipment go along with this leisure identity? Are some things required and some luxury items?

Does this leisure identity have a specific language or terms that need to be learned in order to have a dialogue with others sharing the same identity? How was this language learned?

How has looking the part contributed to your sense of belonging?

Competencies

> *You do not need to be a Rembrandt to consider yourself an artist,*
> *or a Wayne Gretsky to be a passionate hockey player.*
> *The joy is in the striving.*

Leisure is about doing and venturing. There are no truly passive leisure pursuits. Following our dreams and going after our passions in leisure always requires scheming and planning and taking action. There are also no leisure pursuits that do not necessitate some level of competency. Competency is related to having an adequate skill level with which to function and/or participate. Although we often think about it in terms of fluency and mastery, competency does not demand the two.

Each leisure role and related identity requires learning basic competencies. The initial stage of the learning curve is concerned with figuring out the minimal requirements of the role or what it takes to participate. The next stage involves practising and polishing these basic skills until some basic level of competency is achieved which enables us to partici-

pate. Once we are able to do some of the basic skills required to participate, we can decide whether or not to go further and work at excelling
or achieving higher levels of mastery, or whether we are comfortable
with the skill level we have achieved. Many individuals are satisfied with
reaching basic levels of competence, while others strive for further mastery and personal excellence.

The question of how competent we must become before we are willing or
able to define ourselves in terms of a particular leisure identity (e.g. I am a guitar
player) or decide on the level of competency we want to achieve is extremely
individualistic. It seems to depend on a number of factors including:

Potency :	How important is this leisure identity to my sense of who I am? How important is this leisure identity in terms of my overall role spectrum? How passionate am I about this role and individualizing it?
Accomplishment :	How accomplished am I in other roles in my life? How much do I feel a need to be accomplished in this area? How confident and secure am I in other roles? How important is it to me to achieve some level of mastery?
Expectation :	What external role expectations have I internalized for the particular role e.g. you must be as good as your parent before you can call yourself a chess player...or you must be sure you are enjoying yourself first and foremost. What internal expectations have I placed on myself for this role?
Investment :	What resources am I willing to make available for investing in the leisure pursuit? – time, money, energy, commitment...
Complexity :	How difficult is it for me to develop skill fluency and mastery? How complex are the role expectations?
Motivations & Abilities :	How motivated and passionate am I about learning the skills required? How much effort, discipline, and/or sacrifice is required to adapt and/or accommodate the pursuit to my particular abilities and aptitudes?

There is a complicated interaction between how others define us and
how we define ourselves. While it seems obvious that the judgments of
others are affected by our own self-definition, it is also true that self-def-
initions are influenced by the perceptions of others. For some people,
competency is critical to self-definition while others rely more on image
and whether they feel the part. Still others are far more interested in
allowing the identity to emerge as a true expression of themselves and
grow over time.

Building competencies and achieving mastery in certain leisure identities can offer a strong sense of accomplishment that may or may not be
obtainable from other realms in our lives like work and community. Com-

petency can also act as a source of status among our peers, assist in identifying our gifts and building reputations in our communities.

For persons with disabilities, the issue of building competencies in the community while participating in leisure alongside their peers has been a thorny one. The traditional model in leisure service delivery has been based on a continuum model. This model has been widely interpreted to mean that individuals should learn the skills that are required to participate in a leisure pursuit in a sheltered setting. This form of segregation was justified on the basis that individuals must have the skills and "be made ready" before they were put to the test in the real world.

It is clear from the pioneering efforts in integrated leisure services, that individuals need to learn while participating alongside their non-handicapped peers so that they can feel and be part of the dynamic leisure experience. It has been found over and over again that the best learning ground for anyone is the "real world" because it offers rich and diverse learning models and compelling reasons for participation. By zeroing in on an individual's passions the compelling reasons for learning are present and the learning curve is often accelerated (Hutchison and McGill 1992).

> *It is good to have an end to journey towards,*
> *but it is the journey that matters in the end.*
>   Ursula LeGuin

Some Questions for Reflecting:

What kinds of skills/competencies have you learned from your leisure identity?

What other things have you learned about life in general from your leisure involvement?

What skills have you learned that are not directly related to the leisure identity?

What skills have you mastered? Have you been recognized for this mastery in any way? How?

Which skills do you wish to achieve mastery in? How important is mastering certain skills to you?

Rhythms and Routines

Various leisure identities have different rhythms and routines associated with them. We are naturally attracted to those leisure interests that have rhythms and routines that best fit with our lifestyles and personalities.

Some leisure identities have a strict discipline and routine associated with them. They may even require a daily regimen of activity to achieve certain levels of minimum proficiency. For example, in certain styles of yoga practice, students are expected to be committed to daily workouts that commence at daybreak and go through two hours of stretching and chanting rituals. In this solitary pursuit, missing a day of practice is viewed as a minor setback.

Other leisure identities require intense involvement for short periods of time and allow for long periods of dormancy between participation. This is true of being an actor in amateur theatre productions. In this rhythm, there is intense involvement during auditions and rehearsals that is brought to a crescendo with three or four nights of performance. This rhythm is suitable to individuals who do not enjoy or who are not able to give sustained focussed attention to a leisure identity all year round. This "short burst" high intensity involvement is very attractive to some individuals.

Still other leisure identities have a strong inherent rhythm like the art of weaving where the artist is constantly switching between the warp and the weft to create a rich interplay of colours and textures. The rhythm is felt by the artist and built into the activity itself and yet it does not dictate the rhythm of participation. Weavers can leave their work sitting for days or even months on the loom before they start up again, without affecting the quality. This sporadic intensity and inherent rhythm is what makes weaving attractive to other individuals.

Some leisure identities are influenced by seasonal rhythms and weather conditions. Golf is a prime example of a seasonal leisure pursuit that is strongly influenced by weather conditions. If you live in Canada or in other snowy climates, golf courses are only open for five or six months of the year. Throughout the rest of the year, golfers must make do with their memories, trips to the south, golf magazines and television. Efforts are being made to mediate these natural rhythms by building indoor driving ranges and golf courses, however these settings change the golf experience quite dramatically and for that reason are only attractive to some golfers.

Some Questions for Reflecting:

What impact does your leisure identity have on your work? Does it demand flexible work hours, does it complement work, does it have related skills?

Are there certain times of year that your involvement in your passion is more intense than others? If so, what do you do to maintain the passion during the "off season" periods or times when it is not as easy to participate?

What kind of rhythm and routine are you most attracted to and why?

Leisure Identity Development and Maintenance

Young children are initially exposed and attracted to different leisure interests through imitation and modelling. Parents and sometimes other family members are the primary role models. Young children want to try out what their parents and older siblings are doing. They are motivated to participate initially by a desire to explore as well as a need to fit in and belong.

Parents play a critical role in a child's leisure development by offering either encouragement or discouragement. It is their commitment to helping their children explore their own interests that lays the foundation for a passive or active leisure lifestyle as an adult. Many parents are conscious of letting their children try out a broad repertoire of leisure pursuits starting first with those interests they are most familiar with and gradually moving to things that the child seems either to prefer or show some interest in. As well, a lot of parents consciously make an effort to expose their children to leisure activities that they themselves enjoyed as children or those activities that have been passed down through the generations from their own parents.

In the early years, and even into adolescence, parents typically act as "leisure coordinators" for their children. They facilitate their leisure by taking them here and there, registering them for various activities, encouraging this activity over that. At these stages, parents play a significant role in decision-making, by deciding which activities to invest in financially and emotionally. For this reason, the parents' leisure passions strongly influence a child's early choices. As children mature, however, they are drawn to activities that they see modelled by other children their own age and activities that they themselves are truly passionate about.

Typically, as adults, we can reflect on our childhoods as a time of leisure exploration or even leisure identity development. We can draw on these experiences, re-discovering them as adults. This is not necessarily true for many people with disabilities. For them, childhood has often been a time of isolation rather than exploration, and it is difficult for them to draw on past experiences as a way of forming an opinion on what they would like to do now.

Even when we are adults, our families of origin often continue to support and encourage us, and help connect us to others they meet that share a similar passion. That is, if they feel that it is a worthwhile pursuit and has not meant too much sacrifice on their part. For example, when an involvement has led to an inordinate amount of sacrifice on the part of family members, as sometimes happens in highly competitive sports identities, there may be an unwillingness to continue offering support to an adult son or daughter.

There are others that support us in developing leisure identities as adults. Our lovers, spouses and intimate others play a critical role in providing support and encouragement. This encouragement can come in many different forms – praise, support to take courses, financial support to purchase materials and equipment and simply appreciation and recognition for what we have become. On the other hand, it can be in our most intimate relationships that we witness the least support and encouragement for pursuing our passions. Sometimes, the sacrifices and investments that individuals want to make are seen as too great on the part of the spouse, lover or family members.

Community friends and co-workers also play a role in affirming us in our leisure identities. When they take the time to get to know who we are in each of the realms in our lives they are affirming our whole being. When they limit their view of us as one thing or another and don't take the time to see us in our fullness we feel somehow diminished. This feeling of being negated or not recognized for our wholeness is a common experience of persons with handicapping conditions.

Some Questions for Reflecting:

How did you become initially attracted to and interested in each of your leisure identities?

Was there someone in particular who "showed you the ropes?"

How has your identity been supported in the past and how is it now being supported by others?

In what ways do others encourage and or discourage the identity? i.e., emotional, financial or physical support (or lack thereof)?

What skills and competencies related to the identity have people taken the time to teach you?

When did you first begin to perceive yourself differently as a result of your leisure identity? e.g. you began to call yourself a golfer or a gardener or a dancer....

What triggered this change in your self-perception?

Process: Working it Through

Getting Started

Throughout the demonstration project, the overall process focussed on getting to know the person casually over a period of time to uncover his or her leisure patterns, passions and dreams. By establishing a relationship with individuals, and at times with their families, the task of determining which particular leisure roles they would like to focus on was made more natural. Information was usually gathered informally in conversation or by observing the individual in action. It was extremely helpful for leisure support workers or family members and friends to do the exercises and answer the questions about their own leisure first. This allowed them to gain some personal insight into the process before they began to support someone else through it.

Establishing the Past and Current Circumstances

Staff met with most of the individuals several times initially, to get to know them. It was important to get together with people casually over a meal or while going out to participate in some kind of activity. This not only helped build trust, but also set a tone that was different from other "agency programs." Staff gathered information from the individuals and at times from their families and friends about their past and current leisure involvements through informal discussions and observations. They asked individuals to take them to the places in their communities they had become most familiar with. Many of these places were related to their leisure: shopping malls, parks, bowling alleys. Individuals talked about the people in their lives and whom they enjoy doing things with. Staff worked at gaining an understanding of each person's social network, whom they knew and felt most close to. Some individuals told staff about their lives by showing them their personal photo albums. This worked particularly well for people who did not express themselves verbally.

Throughout the early stages of the process staff took time to note any dreams that emerged from discussions with the individuals and/or their families.

The questions in Table Three communicate the kinds of information we found to be essential. This is not to suggest that formal questionnaires or extensive questioning processes would be particularly helpful. In fact, they would be detrimental to getting at the essence of a person's leisure lifestyle. These are questions to be held in mind, rather than asked directly. Through our work with the individuals involved in the project, each of the questions was answered in its own time.

Table Three
Reflections on Your Leisure

PAST PREFERENCES

What kinds of leisure activities have you participated in, in the past that you thoroughly enjoyed? Did not like at all? Why?

PASSIONATE INVOLVEMENTS

What do you do in your leisure now, that you are passionate about? What is it that you love to do, and would love to spend more time doing if you could?

When was the last time you did what you are most passionate about? What keeps you from it?

What do you do in your leisure that gives you meaning, that you feel truly excited about?

Do you have a leisure identity currently? Is it strong or emerging? Who supported its development, and how? In what areas have you built competencies?

Has there ever been another time in your life where you were passionately involved in a leisure pursuit and had a leisure identity? If so, what was it and how did it feel?

MEANING

What meaning do you give to your current leisure experiences? i.e., "My leisure, helps me to reconnect with things I enjoyed as a child."

DESCRIBING YOURSELF IN YOUR LEISURE

When you are asked to describe what you do in your leisure, how do you describe yourself? In terms of things you've tried before, events you've attended, what you do on a regular basis, what you're passionate about or is it in terms of what your preferences are? "I am a home body, I like to stay home and read with a nice cozy blanket."

Have these descriptors changed over time? Have there been times when you would have hesitated to refer to yourself in terms of your leisure identity? or times when your leisure identities seemed much more in the forefront?

What other roles do you have in work, family, community...

LEISURE ACTIVITIES

What leisure activity do you participate in now that would not be considered a passion?

How would you describe your leisure? Are you satisfied or dissatisfied with your current leisure?

LEISURE TIME

What time do you set aside for your leisure? Is there any specific time that you consider sacred, that no-one can tamper with, or is your leisure time wedged in whenever you find some space amongst all of your other obligations and commitments?

PATTERN OF INVOLVEMENT

Is there a regular pattern of involvement? " I go to the gym twice a week without fail."

Is there a more irregular pattern – something that you do sporadically or when the mood strikes, when the supports are put into place or when everything else falls into place?

MOTIVATIONS

What is the single largest motivating factor in your leisure participation? What are you looking for? What do you want to get out of your involvement?

BENEFITS

What do you seem to be getting out of your current leisure experiences? What benefits do you derive from your leisure?

RELATIONSHIPS

Who do you generally participate with in your leisure? Is there any kind of pattern about who you spend time with?

Who is in your personal social network? Have these individuals introduced you to any particular leisure interests?

Who do you already know who shares your particular passion?

ACTION SPACE

What is your action space or where do you go regularly?

What spaces and places are you most familiar with?

Do you get to these places on your own or with support?

FACILITIES AND RESOURCES

What leisure facilities and/or resources are you most familiar with?

What leisure facilities are close to your home or work?

SUPPORT

Who gives you support both formally and informally to pursue your passions and/or participate in leisure? Family, friends, staff?

What form of support do you receive? Financial, emotional, moral, informational, educational, physical, transportation, or any other form?

FAMILIAL PATTERNS

Do you still have close or substantial ties to family members?

What are your family of origin's leisure patterns ? How have these patterns/habits influenced you? How do they still influence you?

Are there any family cultural or ethnic traditions that have had an influence on your leisure participation? That you would give anything to take up again?

LIFE CYCLE

What stage are you in your life cycle? What impact does this have on your leisure patterns, preferences and passions? "I am just about to leave home and I am looking at what to do when I am on my own and how to meet new people."

Dreaming
Establishing the Dream and the Vision

> *Dreams are the butterflies of the soul.*
> *Delicate, carefree and elusive,*
> *taking wing, alighting and resting.*
> *Gracefully moving us to where we ought to be.*

Our dreams for ourselves are always with us. We tuck them away and protect them from those we feel might trample on them. Our dreams represent the images of ourselves that we cherish and hold most dear. For that reason, we need to treat them with immense gentleness and respect. Dreams speak to our vision of the future and our own possibilities. Allowing ourselves to dream aloud is like opening the door to the future and peering into what might be in store for us.

> *I have spread my dreams under your feet.*
> *Tread softly because you tread on my dreams.*
>
> W.B. Yeats

Many of the individuals and families supported by the Brampton Caledon project were full of hopes and dreams that they had submerged over time. The task was to breathe life into those dreams, hopes and passions that they had lost touch with or had chosen to keep quiet and guard close to their hearts. It was to assist individuals to develop an imagination for their own "possibilities." It was about getting in touch with what the person had dreamed about before he or she had stopped letting others know about those dreams.

Expressing hopes and dreams is not an easy process for a lot of people. For most, it meets with a lot of resistance. This is partly because we have become accustomed to only asking for what we think we are likely to get. As well, there is considerable vulnerability related to sharing our secret desires and dreams for ourselves or our children. There is the possibility that we will be ignored or worse, not taken seriously. As well, some families have experienced outright rejection when they stated their dreams because others felt the dreams were not realistic or even desirable. For this reason, project workers were conscious of the need to clearly express their intention to honour whatever the individuals and/or families told them. Due to this commitment to people they needed to stay really conscious of their own prejudices and biases as leisure support workers.

From the beginning, they let people know they would try to help them go after whatever passions or wishes they expressed. For the leisure support workers, this meant staying really conscious of their own prejudices and biases. It was all too easy to put a damper on a passion that someone expressed. As well, when confronted by individuals who were still lacking an imagination for what they might do and could not think of one thing they would like to pursue, the natural urge was to start them on something the leisure support workers knew well. While this may be a starting point, it cannot replace the dreaming process. In these situations, support persons must recognize themselves as the source of the inspiration and be sure that, over time, they are taking their cues from the individual and enabling them to assume more of a role in decision making.

> *Go confidently in the direction of your dreams.*
> *Live the life you've imagined.*
>
> Henry David Thoreau

Many of the individuals' dreams involved their wishes to be reunited with the people in their lives from whom they had become disconnected, to maintain current relationships or to develop new ones. This is not surprising, given the close connection between relationship building and leisure, and the potential of leisure to foster relationships. These dreams were taken seriously and whenever possible, leisure was used as the context for the interaction.

Leisure support workers found that the traditional, assessment-oriented methods for determining what someone really wanted to do in their leisure were too "dispassionate". They rarely led to people "letting the cat out of the bag" or sharing a highly cherished wish. For this reason, we developed a series of questions and exercises that, over time and through observation and/or discussion helped people to open up.

While participating alongside people and while doing dreaming sessions it was important for leisure support workers to be sensitive to how and when individuals expressed their passions. At times it was appropriate and possible to ask certain questions to help stimulate discussions and get people feeling free to speak about the visions they held for themselves. At other times, it was best and more effective to glean the information through close observation. The following questions provided a focus throughout the process, whether asked directly or borne in mind during observation:

Table Four
Discovering Your Passions

- What lights you up?
- What do you spend a lot of your time anticipating and getting excited about?
- When do you seem most focussed and unaware of distractions?
- When do you seem and feel most alive?
- What helps you feel a sense of purpose?
- What gets you animated?
- What inspires you to talk and get excited?
- Do you remember a time when you really felt proud of yourself? What were you doing at the time?
- When was a time that you felt at peace with yourself? What was happening?
- Have you ever been doing something and then realized that a lot of time had passed? What were you doing?
- Is there a time in your leisure when you can remember smiling a lot and feeling really happy? Describe that time.
- What do you do that really makes you smile, laugh and feel happy inside?
- What do you remember doing in your leisure that made you stand up tall and feel really good about yourself?
- What have you tried in your leisure that you would give anything to try again?
- If you had lots of money, what would you want to do with it? Where would you go and what would you buy?
- What was your favorite thing to do as a child? Why was it your favourite thing? Who did you do it with?
- If you had all the time in the world, how would you spend it, and who would you spend it with?
- Is there anything that you used to do a lot of in your leisure that you would love to take up again?
- As a child, what did your family do together for leisure, on weekends and during vacations? With relatives?
- As a child, what did your family do together for leisure, with relatives?
- What does your family do together now?
- What is something you have always wanted to do in your leisure but were afraid to try?
- When are you most proud of yourself? How does it feel?
- What hidden talent do you have that no one but you seems to know about?
- If you could be someone special in your leisure who would you be?

Table Four (cont'd)

- Did you ever see someone doing something on television that you wanted to learn to do yourself?
- Do you know of any neighbours/family members/friends/staff that have interesting hobbies or who do interesting things with their spare time? What makes it interesting to you?
- Who is your idol? Why is he or she your idol, what is it about him/her that you admire?
- If you were to go on a trip, where would you go and what would you do? Whom would you take with you?
- Would you like to become a member of a club or organization? Which club or what kind of club? How do you know about that club? What do you think it would be like to be a member of that group? What would make that fun?

The exercise on the next page focuses us on those things in our life that we love, that stir our passions and that give us hope. This exercise proved useful for getting individuals and their families to think creatively during the dreaming sessions. It can be completed by an individual alone, in partners, or with support. At times family and friends did the exercise to express what they knew about what the individual most loves.

For individuals who cannot write down or articulate their ideas easily, the list of questions can be used as a series of prompts to assist discussion. For individuals who do not communicate verbally, it can be used as a list of things that can be carefully watched for by support person/s.

"All the Things You Love" Exercise

Write a list, or have your partner take down your list of all the things you love in the world:

all the things you love to see, touch and smell; all the people you love and all the things you do or have done or would love to do, all the things that give you pleasure, a sense of inner peace, a feeling of exhilaration; all the things that remind you of your calling or purpose, that make you feel secure and content, that fill you with wonder, that spark your imagination, that conjure up the playful side of you, that encourage your spontaneous nature, that get you in touch with nature, that fill you with hope.

What do your answers to these questions tell you about yourself, your current situation, your hopes and dreams? What do your answers tell you about your rhythms, where you find beauty, what restores and rejuvenates you, what spurs you on in life, what brings you back to your centre, what is essential and non-essential in your life, what you need to begin looking at again in your life, where your passion is, and which leisure interests are most ripe for pursuing?

Limiting Forces and Assumptions

There are several traps we fall into at times. Some stop us from dreaming on our own behalf, and going beyond our daily rhythm and routine, while others stop us from taking action on our dreams for ourselves. Sometimes it is fear that keeps us in a holding pattern, unable to take the risks required to make changes that would put us on a different path, while other times it is not believing in ourselves.

For people who have been devalued, and for their families, these fears are even more real, more devastating. Individuals and their families have been "programmed" to think small and to lower their expectations for achievement drastically. Individuals have been conditioned to believe that their lives will remain predictable. They will stay in the same place and work at the same job. Staff may come and go but routines will remain the same. Many people with disabilities have learned to cope with the discontinuity of relationships in their lives by clinging to the security of knowing what was coming next.

Taking risks and breaking the everyday routines was challenging for the people involved in the project. So too was taking action on their dreams. They had grown accustomed to having things done for them and being told what to do next. The project offered a chance to break that pattern and to begin truly directing their own support and their leisure. Many of the individuals began thoroughly enjoying the opportunity to venture into new experiences, while others felt threatened by the freedom of it.

> *People with high self esteem have it*
> *because they have overcome their failures.*
> *They have been put to the test of life,*
> *overcome the problems and grown.*
>
> David Jansen

There are traps that make dreaming difficult for all of us, and especially for those who are devalued by the culture. Some of these are set out in Table Five on the next page.

Table Five
Traps That Make Dreaming Difficult:

- losing faith in our dreams
- feeling trapped by poverty, instead of budgeting and figuring out how certain things might be done affordably
- fear of "becoming" or venturing into a "new me"
- losing the willingness and capacity to risk and take a chance
- asking others for what we think we can get – not what we really want
- doing what is expected of us rather than what we really want to do
- being unwilling to say what it is we really want in life
- expecting the reoccurrence of rejection from social groups; believing that community groups are not going to be welcoming to us
- holding minimal expectations for our own personal growth and being afraid to look for meaning and purpose in our lives
- believing that enjoyment in all leisure pursuits is based on competence and skill, and that we must already have the skills before they can be enjoyable
- having stability and security as the ultimate goal and ruling ourselves out of experiences that could dramatically change our lives
- putting ourselves in a waiting pattern: waiting for retirement; waiting for life to stabilize; waiting for parents to die ("I'll get married when my parents die, I don't want to disobey their wishes.")
- believing that, as a client my job is to make staffs' jobs easier and in leisure that means signing up for programs and doing whatever diversionary activity comes my way

Taking Action

> *Whatever you can do*
> *or dream you can,*
> *begin it.*
> *Boldness has genius,*
> *magic and power in it.*
> *Begin it now.*
>
>   Goethe

An essential stage of all dreaming is the point at which we begin to take action and transform the dream into reality. This stage is difficult for everyone because it requires coming face to face with our fears and limitations. It is the stage where we must deal with both our commitment to the alternative vision of ourselves and our faith that it is possible. We must come to terms with how committed we are to carrying through with our dreams. We must struggle with not only how much faith we have in ourselves, but also how much faith we have that others will be there for us and help us to make our dreams come true. Finally, it is about our will force. The will force represents our drive and determination to pursue a particular goal or desire. In taking action the question becomes, do we have the will force to go on an entirely new journey of self and recreate our lives?

Throughout the course of the project it was necessary to use a number of methods for facilitating the dreaming process. For those individuals and families that had not been able to define a clear focus through the dreaming exercises and discussions presented earlier, staff introduced a process described in Elaine Dembe's book *Passionate Longevity* (1995). In the book she describes how David Talbot, a management consultant, uses a dreaming process that helps participants face their fears and create concrete action plans. Talbot's process was adapted for the purpose of this project. For some individuals this process was not appropriate or useful because it requires considerable visual and abstract thinking. For others, it provided a means for activating their imaginations and a way to become more fully engaged in dreaming.

Dreaming into the Future Exercise:

The "dreamer" is asked to dream aloud. The "dream facilitator" or support person either records it with a tape recorder or writes what the dreamer says as fully and completely as possible .

Dream facilitator:

Pick a time in the future, when you are happier than you ever thought you could be. You are completely fulfilled and love all the things you're doing. What date is it?

The dreamer gives a specific date, like April 11th 2001.

Dream facilitator:

Zero in on this time and imagine that many of the dreams you have set for yourself have come true. Allow yourself to really get a picture of it, feel it. Describe what your life looks like.

At this point the dreamer begins to describe what he or she sees in the future. When the person runs out of images the dream facilitator can ask further questions to keep the images flowing freely. The dream facilitator must be careful not to interrupt or judge when people are giving images. They must encourage people to give as much detail as they can and to build images as vividly as they can.

These questions can be helpful:

What does your life feel like?

Who is in your life? Are there any new people?

What are you doing?

Where are you in the dream?

What does that place look like? Is there anything familiar in that place? Is there anything strange in that place?

How do you spend your time? Do you work? What do you do in your leisure?

What do you love doing?

How do you know you are happy? How can you tell?

What have you bought for yourself?

How have others around you changed?

What are you looking forward to?

What plans have you been making?

What details do you notice in the dream?

What are you nervous about?

If you could speak in your dream what would you say?

What have you accomplished?

Dream facilitator:

Return to the present, relax and listen as I read back or play back your dream to you. How do you feel about what you hear? What did you learn about yourself? What part of the dream are you most excited about? What are the things in the dream that you want to come true? Which parts of the vision are you most excited about? (Record the responses. Encourage the responses to be as specific as possible.)

Tell me all the reasons the dream cannot come true. Why do you feel it is unrealistic? What are your worst fears when you think about your dream? What would make it go sour? What would ruin it all?

(Ensure that the dreamer is being as specific as possible throughout the process. Record all of the person's misgivings, fears and worries, barriers, obstacles that are expressed without making any comments.)

The facilitator now works with the dreamer to draw out the common themes and patterns in these comments, e.g. I hear that you are really feeling insecure about living on your own. Is that correct?

List a few of the major obstacles to the dream becoming reality.

For each theme or obstacle, have the individual on their own or with support come up with three or four concrete "do-able" action steps that they could take or that could be taken, to overcome them.

Review the list of action steps and figure out how the plan can be implemented. What kinds of supports are already in place, what supports need to be called upon, what leisure roles have been highlighted for taking action?

When the process is used with individuals, it is possible to use the format above. When it is used with family members or friends substitute the person's name, or your brother/sister, son/daughter ... for the word "you".

(Adapted from David Talbot in *Passionate Longevity*)

Support Strategies:
Striking the Right Balance

The information gained through our initial observations, discussions and dreaming processes gave a starting point for providing support. We began developing each person's support strategy by making a list of experiences and activities that he or she seemed to be most interested in exploring and choosing one or two leisure roles to focus on.

For some individuals the next step was to assist them to get out and explore the activities they had asked to learn more about. For these individuals, having an opportunity to try things out seemed enough. It was certainly what they were used to. They held very little expectation for themselves to go beyond "one shot" trials of activities. When staff expressed an interest in knowing which activities the individuals liked most, and wanted to pursue, they were met with a lot of bafflement. Individuals involved in the project were not used to this approach. They were also not used to the intensity of support that staff were willing to provide in order to help them make things happen in their lives. They were cynical about staff's willingness to support them to go further. It was very clear that many of them had been part of other "pilot" initiatives and knew the kinds of discontinuities that had been created in their lives. These individuals viewed their participation in the project as having been given a "treat." They saw themselves as being more fortunate than some of the other people being served by the agency who were not part of the project. They did not want to hope for too much. Over time, these barriers dissolved and individuals began trusting in the project's objectives. For others, the idea of getting ongoing support was a real relief. They were able to jump in with both feet and begin directing their support and formulating where they would go next.

Once an individual's interests were identified, staff began exploring them with the person to see if there were one or two that really seemed like a focus or primary interest. For some individuals it was very clear from the beginning that they wanted to focus on a certain role. For others, there seemed to be a cluster of interests that had a central theme to them. For example, one of the men was interested in all activities that involved military-like adventure. Some of the individuals could identify only general trends and directions at first. From these general themes we gained ideas for activities to explore.

At times staff felt that they were groping around in the dark trying to get some inkling of where an individual's passion lay, and where the focus was. As they continued to support individuals however, and worked at staying aware of the subtle shifts that were taking place, it always became clear when a true passion had begun to emerge.

The Element of Discovery

Once an individual had found a focus or a broad leisure role to pursue, staff tried to be available to them to provide support and assistance as they discovered the many aspects of the role. It was also time to bring other people together to begin asking some basic support questions including:

How does leisure fit into your overall dreams for yourself?

What will it take for you to reach some of the dreams you have spoken of?

What are you most afraid of?

How can these fears be addressed and action still be taken?

What kind of support is necessary to make these dreams happen?

What are some possible strategies to try initially and over time?

How intense will the supports need to be initially and over time?

Who should be involved initially in providing support?

Who else could be involved initially in providing support?

What kind of support might be needed over the long run?

How can you guide the support?

Having individuals be in charge of their support and their own process of discovery was critical. As we discover our passion(s) in leisure, we do it at our own pace and in our own time. This rhythm is important and must be honoured. As staff, and sometimes as family members, it is too easy to take control of finding the resources and "getting everything set up" in advance for the individual. This "fix it" approach simply dissolves the passion and blocks the "will drive" to pursue it. It is precisely what we are trying to go beyond by supporting individuals to "become" in their leisure.

Even though intense supports were often required initially by the individuals, it was important to allow this aspect of exploration and discovery to be as organic and free-flowing and as free from routine as possible. This meant that for people who knew very little about their interests, staff would let them slowly discover aspects of it in their own time. They would assist individuals to find certain resources if they asked for them, or if they seemed to be asking through their behavior and/or actions. For example, someone who was going trail riding on a regular basis and seemed content to do so was not taken out to find out about horseback riding lessons, until he started asking questions about lessons and had refused to leave the stable because he wanted to learn how to groom the horses himself.

Staff either assisted individuals to find out the information themselves or gave them information in such a way that they could then make the choices. This isn't to suggest that people were left to flounder, but staff did hold the expectation that individuals would tell them in some way when they were interested in finding out more, doing more or discovering more. The intention was to follow their lead and assist them to discover the next piece of information or resource. Staff were there to support individuals in taking action to fulfil their dreams.

It must be pointed out that "intense supports" are not ones that smother or that treat individuals as if they were in need of a bodyguard, someone to shadow them, or keep them out of trouble. Intense support means ensuring that individuals are given, or are assisted to find what they need to participate in a meaningful way. Supports must be relevant, flexible and timely. For instance, if someone needs support to go country line dancing every Friday night and that means assistance to get to the bar and get home again, then that is the kind of support that should be provided. If staff or family members can only be available to them on a Saturday night, once every three months, and are not willing to figure out another way of getting them there on a regular basis, then the available support is irrelevant. More relevant supports must be looked at and created to make it happen. Intense support is relevant support.

Developing Visual Maps of the Role and Identity

The process of assisting an individual to develop an identity is inevitably slow. Once staff got involved in supporting individuals to explore activities and to begin to develop a focus they felt a need to become and remain conscious of the subtle shifts that were taking place. The process requires so much attention to subtleties that it was easy to feel at times that nothing had really changed in the person's life. Drawing visual maps assisted enormously in paying attention to the subtle ways in which the individual was beginning to explore the role and express the identity. Visual maps were also used to reveal areas where we might be able to provide more intentional support.

By drawing up a map every once in a while throughout the process staff were able to become conscious of the shifts that were taking place in each person. There were shifts in a number of areas:

- self-perception
- anticipation of an activity – can't wait to do it again
- relationships
- eagerness and willingness to develop a focus and get intensely involved in something
- awareness of the language of the role – e.g. "golf talk"
- skills and competencies
- awareness of the "image" related to their role – "dress like a golfer"
- awareness of their community – where to go to find others who are interested in the same thing
- how others began to see and define them
- what they talked about in their conversations with others
- their general physical and emotional health

The visual maps were tools that helped guide support and give information about the process of discovery the person was going through. They were not intended to be prescriptive in any way, or to imply "this is what you have to do next."

Mapping the Broad Leisure Role

Early in each individual's planning process, the leisure support workers drew a broad leisure role map of the interest(s) they had identified as a focus. These maps were often drawn when staff were together as a team in order to benefit from each other's experiences. In families, these maps were drawn with as many people involved as possible. Drawing the map enabled family and staff to become more conscious of the various aspects of the role and of the multitude of possibilities and resources available within the community. By becoming more conscious and expanding their personal vision of what the role could involve and what it could mean for an individual, they began the process of confronting personal biases and ignorance related to each role.

Throughout the process family members and staff tried to ensure that their ambivalence or dislike for an activity did not put a damper on the dreams and wishes of the people included in the project. Mapping the broad leisure role was an intentional way of dealing with the built-in biases and prejudices each of us held about certain passions. By mapping the leisure role we came to understand it a bit more, what it involves and how people come to cherish it. Connecting the individuals with others in the community who shared the passion also went a long way toward lessening the impact of our biases and keeping the flame alive in the individuals.

By drawing this map, the support persons often came to realize how little they knew about certain interests. They also recognized how unconscious they had been about many aspects of those interests they were more familiar with. The mapping process helped them to open up to the complexity and diversity of various leisure roles. The maps evolved to encompass our new understandings of the roles, their subtleties and their possibilities.

An example of a broad leisure role map is provided on the next page.

BUY RADIO SCANNERS
THAT ALLOW YOU TO LISTEN
TO AIR TRAFFIC CONTROLLERS

CAN IDENTIFY VARIOUS
AIRCRAFT BY MAKE
AND CARRIER – CIVILIAN
AND MILITARY

GET PILOT LICENSE
TO FLY SMALL AIRCRAFT

READ ADVENTURE BOOKS
ABOUT WARPLANES – AND
THE HERO PILOTS

USE FLIGHT SIMULATORS – ON
COMPUTERS AND THE
REAL ONES PILOTS TRAIN ON

READ BOOKS
ON AIRCRAFT

LEARN ABOUT FAMOUS
MILITARY AIRCRAFT
AND THEIR PILOTS

SUBSCRIBE TO VARIOUS
NEWSLETTERS ABOUT
THE AIR CARRIER INDUSTRY

GET AN AIRCRAFT
COMMUNICATION
RADIO PILOT LICENSE

GO UP IN SMALL
AIRCRAFT WITH
PILOTS IN TRAINING

Aviation Fan

**Broad Leisure
Role**

TAKE BINOCULARS TO
AIRPORT TO OBSERVE
DETAILS ABOUT AIRCRAFT

STUDY NAVIGATIONAL
METHODS

JOIN PARACHUTE CLUB
AND JUMP FROM PLANES

BECOME A VOLUNTEER
AT SMALL LOCAL AIRPORTS

GET TO KNOW
AVIATION ART
AND ARTISTS

TAKE UP
HOT-AIR
BALLOONING

JOIN RADIO-CONTROLLED
FLYING CLUBS – BUILD YOUR
OWN PLANE – FLY OTHERS'
PLANES AND HELP OUT

TAKE A VIDEO CAMERA
TO THE AIRPORT
AND FILM AIRCRAFT

BECOME KNOWLEDGEABLE
ABOUT THE
SPACE PROGRAM – SPACE
EXPLORATIONS AND SHUTTLES ...

LEARN ABOUT
WEATHER CONDITIONS
– CLOUD FORMATIONS

BUY RECOGNITION
HANDBOOK THAT
DESCRIBES
AIRCRAFT – "JANE'S GUIDE"

LEARN ABOUT EACH
ROLE PLAYED
BY AIR TRAFFIC
CONTROLLERS

BUY AN ULTRALIGHT
AIRCRAFT TO FLY

WATCH AIRCRAFT
TAKE-OFF AND
LAND AT AIRPORTS

GO TO AIR SHOWS
AND EXHIBITS – BOARD
FAMOUS PLANES

CAN IDENTIFY THE VARIOUS
SPECIFICATIONS OF
AIRCRAFT; PAYLOAD,
PASSENGER SIZE, PREVIOUS
CHANGES TO SPECIFICATIONS

TAKE TRIPS THAT
INVOLVE FLYING

DREAM ABOUT BEING
AN AIR TRAFFIC
CONTROLLER

BUILD MODEL
AIRPLANES

BECOME INTERESTED IN
EMPLOYMENT OPPORTUNITIES
AT THE AIRPORT
AND WITH AIRCRAFT

BUY A HAND GLIDER
AND JUMP OFF CLIFFS

VISIT AIRPLANE/
AVIATION MUSEUMS

BUILD AND
FLY KITES

MEET WITH OTHER
AIRPLANE "WATCHERS"
IN ROWS OF CARS
AT THE AIRPORT AND
EXCHANGE KNOWLEDGE
AND TRIVIA ABOUT PLANES

KEEP ON TOP OF INNOVATIONS
AND TECHNOLOGY IN
AIRCRAFT –JET FIGHTERS
AND AIR CARRIERS

STUDY AND LEARN
ABOUT INTERNATIONAL
AIRPORTS

Individual's Initial Map of Leisure Role and Identity

After the broad leisure role map was drawn an initial identity map was drawn to get a sense of how familiar the person was already with the role. The initial identity map also told us how the individual viewed the role, what he or she knew about the possibilities the role might offer and what was most attractive about it.

Identity maps were not drawn from interviews or meetings. They came out of informal discussions and observing people actually participating in the activities.

An example of an initial identity map is shown below.

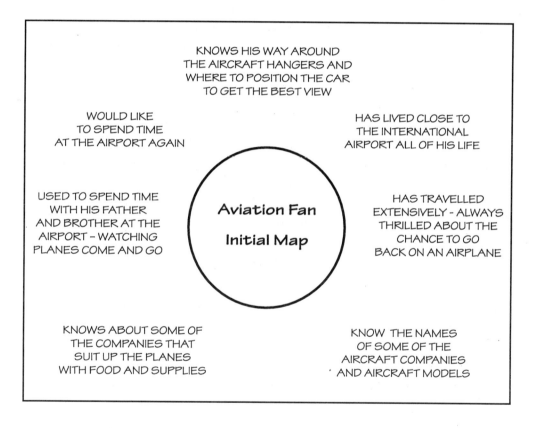

Emerging Identity Map

As each person began to explore more about a leisure role that interested her, it became increasingly evident which aspects of the broad role she found most appealing. Emerging identity maps were drawn throughout the process so that staff could gain a better understanding of how the person's initial interests and awareness had grown, changed and shifted. They also assisted with determining which supports were working or not working and which supports were happening naturally within the community. Emerging identity maps focussed on:

- indicators of the person beginning to "take on the identity;" of actually describing himself in a certain way, insisting on a certain image, or demonstrating a strong will or drive to participate
- likes and dislikes: what gave the individual a thrill about the activity, what he seemed to talk a lot about, or seemed most drawn to about the role
- areas where competencies and image were beginning to be developed; the individual becoming aware of the need to get the right outfit so he could "belong", or wanting to take lessons to become proficient in some area
- relationships: whom they were meeting in the community, how these relationships had arisen and how they were being fostered, encouraged and supported.

In addition, these maps enabled staff to refocus their support and where possible, ask individuals or their families to be more specific about what could be done to help them develop the identity more fully. Useful questions included:

- What would make you feel more like a golfer, a gardener, a karaoke singer?
- What else would you like to explore?
- What is the next step? You have learned this and this, now what else are you wanting to learn?
- Would you like us to introduce you to more people in the community who enjoy this as much as you do?

Examples of three emerging identity maps are provided on the following three pages.

WANTED TO KNOW HOW TO
ZERO IN ON EACH OF THE
AIR TRAFFIC CONTROLLERS RADIO
AIRSPACES TO FOLLOW
THE LANDING AND TAKEOFFS
OF COMMERCIAL JETS

BECAME INTERESTED IN
RADIO-SCANNERS - HOW
MUCH THEY COST AND
HOW TO USE THEM

STARTED TALKING
ABOUT BUILDING
MODEL AIRPLANES

Aviation Fan

Emerging Map #1

WAS WILLING AND
INTERESTED IN GOING
OUT TO THE AIRPORT
ONCE OR TWICE A
WEEK - RAIN OR SHINE

TOOK HIS BINOCULARS
TO GET A BETTER
LOOK AT
COMMERCIAL PLANES

BEGAN GETTING OUT
OF THE CAR AND MEETING
AND EXCHANGING TRIVIA
WITH OTHER PLANE WATCHERS

ASSOCIATED "AIRPLANE
WATCHING" WITH SITTING
IN THE CAR EATING
COFFEE AND DONUTS

.... 2 months later

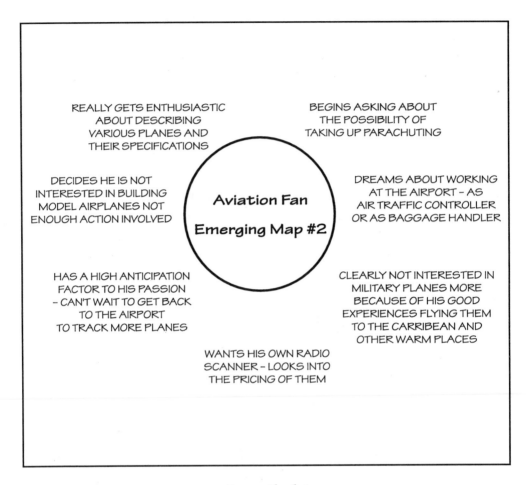

REALLY GETS ENTHUSIASTIC
ABOUT DESCRIBING
VARIOUS PLANES AND
THEIR SPECIFICATIONS

BEGINS ASKING ABOUT
THE POSSIBILITY OF
TAKING UP PARACHUTING

DECIDES HE IS NOT
INTERESTED IN BUILDING
MODEL AIRPLANES NOT
ENOUGH ACTION INVOLVED

Aviation Fan

Emerging Map #2

DREAMS ABOUT WORKING
AT THE AIRPORT – AS
AIR TRAFFIC CONTROLLER
OR AS BAGGAGE HANDLER

HAS A HIGH ANTICIPATION
FACTOR TO HIS PASSION
– CAN'T WAIT TO GET BACK
TO THE AIRPORT
TO TRACK MORE PLANES

CLEARLY NOT INTERESTED IN
MILITARY PLANES MORE
BECAUSE OF HIS GOOD
EXPERIENCES FLYING THEM
TO THE CARRIBEAN AND
OTHER WARM PLACES

WANTS HIS OWN RADIO
SCANNER – LOOKS INTO
THE PRICING OF THEM

.... 5 months later

SAVING MONEY TO BUY
A RADIO SCANNER TO MONITOR
AIR TRAFFIC AND FOLLOW
LANDINGS AND TAKEOFF
PROCEDURES AT THE AIRPORT

LOOKED INTO THE LOCAL
PARACHUTE CLUB AND VISITED
IT TO SEE IF THAT WAS
SOMETHING HE WOULD LIKE
TO DO - STILL UNSURE

GOING THROUGH THE
PROCESS OF FINDING OUT
WHAT IT TAKES TO GET
A JOB AS A
BAGGAGE HANDLER

Aviation Fan

Emerging Map #3

TRYING TO GET INTO
BETTER PHYSICAL
CONDITION IN ORDER TO BE
PREPARED FOR A JOB
AS A BAGGAGE HANDLER

TALKS CONSTANTLY
ABOUT UPCOMING TRIPS
HE IS GOING ON
AND THE LIKELY
AIRCRAFT HE WILL
GET TO FLY IN

GOES TO THE AIRPORT
FREQUENTLY AND IS
STILL LEARNING ABOUT
EACH OF THE
COMMERCIAL AIRCRAFT

WANTS TO BUY THE
BOOK "JANES GUIDE TO
AIRCRAFT RECOGNITION"
TO HELP HIM LEARN MORE

.... 8 months later

"Snapshot in Time" Identity Map

Even though it is obvious that developing a leisure identity is a constantly evolving process, it is useful at times to make a visual map of the identity in its present fullness. This "snapshot in time" map represents an individual's identity as if we could freeze it as a moment in time. By using it as a summary of the overall identity we can get a broader picture of how the person has chosen to interpret the role. We can also gain a better understanding of how the leisure identity has come to play a part in the individual's life.

A "snapshot in time" can look like the map below.

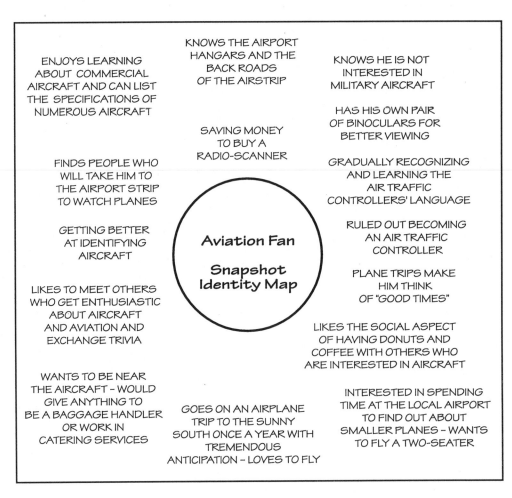

.... 10 months later

Further Support

Throughout the process it was important for staff to think about and/or ask how they could provide further support to individuals. Sometimes this involved thinking about and/or asking individuals, their families and friends questions like:

- "What next?" What would you like to do next to develop this leisure identity?
- What will it take to maintain your passion in this interest?
- What are you afraid might go wrong?
- If you could expand your dream, what would you dream for?
- What is inhibiting your involvement? What keeps you from following your passion? Is it equipment? Are there some things you don't know how to do? Are you having difficulty figuring out creative variations to participation or other ways to do things?
- Who gives you the most support now in following this passion? Are they able to continue this support? Who else might provide this kind of support? Can you be involved without this support? Are there any other possibilities for providing this support?
- Who do you know personally in the community who shares your passion? Are there any organizations which support this leisure interest? What would it take to connect you to these individuals and/or groups?

Reflections on Process

Supporting the development of a person's leisure roles and identities is a difficult process. In many ways, it is strange for us to have to bring so much consciousness to figuring out how an individual begins to really take on a particular identity. We are not used to providing supports in such an intentional way, watching for subtle shifts and discoveries and allowing for a gradual development of competencies. This intentionality and consciousness are critical however, for assisting individuals who have been systematically denied access to valued roles . It helps them to take on a specific identity and to enhance both their image and their competencies related to the leisure identity.

The questions in each of the preceding sections will help when trying to consciously reflect on the way we are or are not providing ongoing leisure support to an individual either as friend, family member or staff person.

Will Forces

The term "will forces" refers to the drive and determination an individual shows for pursuing a particular goal or desire. It is also demonstrated by the amount of persistence that is present in getting something done or in carrying something out.

For example: If someone is "willing" to take two complicated bus connections twice a week to get to her fitness club, she is showing a strong will force and desire to pursue membership in the club. If she missed the bus one night and walked to the next bus stop she would be demonstrating an even stronger example of will force in the form of determination and persistence.

Some Questions for Reflecting

What changes have you noticed in terms of changes in the will force? For example, people taking initiative, wanting to do it no matter what, looking for others with similar interests, finding out more and more about it.

What role does anticipation play in the leisure identity? What are the clues? How was anticipation communicated? Are people thinking, planning, scheming about it?

Does the leisure identity act primarily as an escape? Does the person stay present while participating or is he or she letting his/her attention and interests wander off?

What do you do as a support person, family member or friend that inhibits or blocks the will force in this individual?

How could you support the development of the will force more?

Role of Family Member, Friend or Support Worker

Typically, we are supported in our leisure by our parents, family members and friends. It is only in human services that we even contemplate this role being taken over by or delegated to staff persons. When staff persons take on this role they need to remain aware of how unnatural it is to have a paid staff assist in the area of leisure. Most of us participate in leisure either alone or with family and/or friends. When we venture out into our communities to do things without our family and friends we typically venture out alone, and make new friends and acquaintances ourselves. For this reason, paid staff need to consider as much as possible the many different ways to begin involving other people from the community, including family and friends, in the process. This, and only this, ensures that the person will be supported to maintain the identity over time.

Regardless of who provides the support it must be as intentional as possible. There must also be a willingness to provide support as intensely as necessary especially in the early stages of the identity development.

Some Questions for Reflecting

As a support person, what personal biases, blind spots, prejudices do you have in relation to various leisure pursuits? How do you communicate these directly or indirectly to the people you serve? What challenges do these pose in providing this kind of support?

Which areas of leisure involvements do you feel most insecure and inadequate about? How does this affect your ability to provide support?

Which areas of leisure involvements do you feel most secure, competent and passionate about? What opportunities does this create?

How have these perceptions of competence and incompetence changed over time as you support more individuals in areas you are not familiar with? What has contributed to these changes?

How do you safeguard against bringing your biases to bear on people's choices, dreams and passion? What do you do?

How well connected are you personally to leisure clubs and organizations in the community?

How well connected are you to members of the community, outside the human service world? What are you doing to enhance or strengthen your personal ties to community?

What do you do as friend or support person that serves to strengthen the person's passion?

How has providing leisure support to others shaped the active or dormant leisure identities in yourself?

How has the shared nature of the leisure experiences affected you as the person providing support?

How does the relationship between yourself and the individual foster building relationships with others in the community and how does it foster dependence?

What have you done to link this person up to persons who share a similar passion in the community? What can you do to foster more of these connections? What are your fears in this regard and how have they affected your ability to make the connections?

How do you go about finding others in the community who are closely tied to leisure clubs and associations within the community? How do you foster these connections?

How successful have you been at being able to sit back and take a look at the shifts taking place in a person's self-perception and identity?

How have the leisure patterns of the individual's family affected her leisure involvement? Are there any cultural or ethnic identities within the person's family that have an influence on leisure participation? If so, in what way? How has this affected the kind of support you provide? How have you turned these ethnic and cultural influences into opportunities?
What seems to be motivating the participation of the individual(s) you support? How has this affected the kind of support you provide?

What do the people you support seem to get out of their current leisure experiences?

What meaning do the people you support give to their current leisure experiences? For example "I do this because it gets me out of the apartment, or I like it because I meet new people."

How difficult was it for you to "map" the broad leisure role(s) or what you know already about what the possibilities for a certain role? What made it so difficult?

Relationships

Relationships play an important part in developing leisure identities. Through this process, existing friendships can be strengthened and new ones developed. There is also an important relationship built between the individual and the person(s) providing support.

Some Questions for Reflecting:

What role does relationship-building play in developing this leisure identity? How are the relationships tied in?

How important a factor is finding solid methods of communication in developing this leisure identity? What have you done to ensure that challenges in regard to communication are dealt with and support is provided when necessary?

Who has provided informal support to the individual outside of the planned support?

What indications do you have that some of the people around this person are changing their perceptions of him or her?

How do you know as a support person when to pull back support and when to reach out to other people?

What feedback do individuals generally get from people about whether what they are doing is important or not important to do and whether the amount of energy spent has been and still is worthwhile?

What do I do as a support person that is intentional in terms of helping connect this individual to others who share the same passion?

What more could you do to foster and facilitate good communication between this individual and persons he/she is meeting in the community?

What is left to do? What relationships could still be fostered or nurtured in this person's life?

Self Perception

As individuals grow into a particular role and develop it into an identity, their self-perception begins to shift. These shifts can be fostered in subtle yet supportive ways.

Some Questions for Reflecting

How has the person manifested or taken on the leisure identity in terms of dress, body image, what they own, equipment?

How has the identity shaped the individual's dreams, and plans?

What does the person spend time anticipating and looking forward to?

As you study the maps over time, how has the individual's awareness of the role changed? How much more aware is he of the possibilities related to the leisure role and identity?

What does the individual fear in relation to the involvement? Is it his fear, or that of his parents, friends or the staff?

What other roles and identities influenced the development of the leisure identity both positively and negatively? (Family, work, segregated leisure, client, patient)

Does the person's home reflect anything of the identity? Are others likely to know from visiting the individual what she enjoys and does in her leisure? For example, weight lifting equipment in one of the rooms in the house, or needlepoint cushions on the couch.

Competency

Building competency is an important part of the development of a leisure identity. The more competent we feel, the easier it is for us to see ourselves in a particular role. There is, however, a careful balance to be struck between mastery and basic competency.

Some Questions for Reflecting:

How did the person's involvements foster or build competency? What competencies has the individual already developed?

What relevance does competency have? How competent do people have to become to feel good about the leisure identity, their participation and their enjoyment?

Are some competencies more important to the person's self-perception than others?

Are some competencies more important to other people's perception of the individual in relation to the identity than others?

What kinds of compensatory or adaptive strategies have been useful in assisting the individual to learn the necessary competencies? To participate meaningfully in this activity?

Other Directions

Pursuing a specific leisure identity often opens doors to other related interests. While exploring a leisure identity, it is not uncommon for individuals to discover other interests and to begin exploring and developing them as well. Sometimes these interests can get an individual started on an entirely different path. This kind of exploration is part of the joy of discovering and following your passions.

Precisely because persons with disabilities are used to their leisure experiences being a form of diversion, it may be difficult for them to stay focussed on any particular interest. An individual may be asking for support to pursue a leisure identity and yet be unable to focus. He or she may seem to get caught up diverting his or her time and energy away from it. When this is the case, it is important to discover what the diversion is all about. Sometimes taking up a diversion is natural. It allows all of us to bring balance to our lives when we get too focussed. It may be that the individual is really nervous about the risks involved in pursuing the identity or learning a particular skill. If this is found to be true, then support should be directed at easing the person's trepidation and assisting him to learn the skill in question.

Family members, staff members and friends may also view leisure as a form of diversion and therefore not see the importance of supporting the individual to develop a focussed leisure identity. When staff or family members seem committed to maintaining a certain leisure diversion there is often a long history behind it. When this is the case, it can be useful to gain an understanding of it. This will help support persons to understand what meaning the diversion has for the individual and his or her family or staff. As an example, a 21 year old man was taken regularly by his parents to a petting zoo. His parents felt strongly that the leisure support workers should continue to take him there rather than to the fitness club. For them, the petting zoo was a secure option. It was something he had liked as a child, and was a way for them to spend time with him. Assuring the parents that he really enjoyed the fitness club by telling them stories of his involvements created enough confidence for them to let go of the need for the less age-appropriate diversion.

Some Questions for Reflecting

What other areas/dreams/overlapping interests is the person exploring?

What other interests has this identity opened for the person?

What diverts him or her from staying focussed on certain leisure identities?

What kinds of diversions is the person most interested in? What is the history of these diversions? What role do these diversions play in his/her life?

To what extent are there pressures to rationalize leisure experiences as therapy or "baby-sitting," "busy making" and diversion? Where are these pressures coming from?

Stories

It is easy to believe from reading the following stories that the individuals being supported through the project had few, if any, reasons for needing support. In fact, some readers may fall into the trap of thinking that they had no significant needs at all. This is an extremely interesting perceptional dynamic. We have all become so used to people with disabilities being described and identified primarily by their disability that we become skeptical and confused whenever this is not the case. Perceptions and expectations have extraordinary power, and it is precisely these perceptions and expectations that must change.

The approach we are advocating here is about creating new descriptors of people. It is about supporting individuals to create and maintain valued social roles and to help them to break out of the negative roles they have been placed in and expected to play for so long. This approach is about developing new perceptions of a person's possibilities and gifts.

By describing people positively in terms of who they are becoming, we look at their potential. It allows us to focus support on the positives; what they are learning about themselves and their passion, what they are enjoying, the shifts that are taking place in their lives and how to reach their dreams. It allows space for the identity to emerge and take shape gradually over time. This is crucial for an individual's self-perception to shift.

This approach does not deny the individual's particular vulnerabilities or impairments. These aspects of the individual are still very real. They are taken into consideration at the stage when the individual and family members and support persons begin to ask questions like "What will it take for you to reach this dream? What kind of support is necessary to make this happen, and what are some possible strategies to try initially and over time?" The intensity of the support is established by working through these questions. Knowing about a person's impairment(s) tells us very little about what he wishes and dreams for himself. For this reason, it is essential that we start from the place of dreams and not impairments.

The stories give a small glimpse of a much broader undertaking on the part of the individual and those providing support. They are in no way complete pictures of the development of a leisure identity or what it takes to really make a place for someone in the community. What evolves over a life-time cannot possibly be encapsulated in one story.

The Karaoke Singer

Carol was clear from the very beginning. She wanted support to take part in karaoke evenings at local pubs. She wanted to be a "karaoke regular." The essence of karaoke is to get on stage and sing the vocal part of a song while a compact disc plays the melodies. On stage the karaoke singer has the sensation of being "backed up" by other vocalists and a full band.

Late one night last spring, Carol had her first debut on stage at a hotel bar. She wowed the audience with her raw onstage energy as she danced and sang to one of Madonna's pulsing "bad girl" songs. She held nothing back. It was like she had been singing all her life. This "wild woman" side of Carol came as somewhat of a surprise, given that she is usually so restrained and unassuming in groups.

It hadn't been a total surprise though. Carol's sense of rhythm and love of music had become apparent to staff while she took part in a belly-dancing class. Carol quickly adorned herself with the veils and ribbons that are part of this ancient art and began to shimmer and shake in a tight circle of women who were all trying it out for the first time. Her body was transformed by the Indian music as the group tried to make figure eight shapes with their hips while moving their arms above their heads in rhythmical motions.

As staff and friends began to support Carol to learn about the "karaoke regular" subculture in Brampton, it became clear that her life centred around music. As she sits in the audience during karaoke evenings she is able to name most of the songs and the performers. She knows the lyrics by heart. She is not shy to sing along in the audience and to cheer as people she knows hit the stage. She is undaunted by having her name called to go next. In fact, this is the element she loves most, knowing that it is now her turn in the spotlight, her turn to perform for the audience.

Carol loves to focus on her image. When she is getting ready to go out for a night of karaoke she takes time getting dressed, finding the right look. She also spends a lot of time at home practising her moves, her dances, her delivery of songs.

She has her own karaoke machine at home. She is slowly building up her collection of karaoke tapes. She often videotapes herself performing at home. Carol loves music videos and music television. She sets up taping sessions at home, of music she likes from both radio and television. She has a huge collection of cassette tapes ranging from Madonna and Michael Jackson to Elvis Presley. She likes Madonna because "she is sexy, appealing and kind of Marilyn Munroe-ish."

Elvis Presley is Carol's idol. When asked why, she says it's because "he was good-looking and had lots of money. He wore great suits, he was a real charmer with the ladies, he had good snapping moves and he was famous." She would give anything to visit Graceland some day to get a close-up of his special suits and to take the tour of his mansion.

Recently, Carol participated in a karaoke singing contest. The winner was given the opportunity to make a demo tape at a local recording studio. This was and is the ultimate reward for Carol, to have her singing taken seriously. On the final night, Carol was presented the trophy for most popular singer for the song "Three Times a Lady." This trophy now adorns her dresser. She also won dinner for two at one of her favorite restaurants.

The other karaoke regulars she has met have stage names like Raphael, Queen of Country, R.J. and Rocket Pocket. Having a stage name is a symbol of how serious you are and how conscious you are about creating a stage presence and building a reputation. Carol was slow and methodical in deciding on her stage name. She finally settled on "Queen of Rock and Roll."

Karaoke almost always takes place in bar settings. This does not bother Carol. She sees it as an opportunity to meet people, dance and play pool. In any given evening Carol will submit six songs to sing. She will likely be called on four or five times an evening to appear on stage. Carol knows Suzy Q, one of the main karaoke DJs in town. She has contracts at the various bars and pubs. She has helped introduce Carol to Raphael, R.J. Rocket Pocket and Queen of Country. Carol was invited to attend Suzy Q's wedding last summer and she had a great time. Jacquie, another of the regulars has begun to ask Carol to sit with them during the karaoke. They have exchanged names and phone numbers so that Carol can be kept informed about where Suzy Q will be holding the karaoke the next week.

Being a "karaoke regular" means going out to a bar once or even twice a week; developing a stage name and a specific image; knowing the lyrics and actually practising how you want to perform each song, and entering local and regional karaoke singing contests. For some it means waiting to be discovered. For others it means having fun at it, letting loose and enjoying time in the spotlight.

When asked about the thrill it gives her, Carol says "It's cool because everyone is looking at you and you are in the spotlight. If I could go one hundred times a week, I'd never get bored by it."

BUILD YOUR
CONFIDENCE AND PUT
TOGETHER A "DEMO"
TAPE OF YOUR SINGING
TO TAKE AROUND TO
PRODUCERS

ENJOY THE EXHILARATION
OF SINGING ON STAGE
IN FRONT OF A CROWD

GO REGULARLY AND
DEVELOP AN AUDIENCE
OR "PUBLIC" THAT KNOWS
YOU AND YOUR REPERTOIRE

EXPRESS A PART
OF YOURSELF
NOT EXPRESSED IN
ANY OTHER
CONTEXT

WAITING TO
BE DISCOVERED
OR FIND THEIR
"BIG BREAK"

BUILD A REPUTATION

TRAVEL AROUND TO
KAROKE BARS AND
PARTICIPATE IN
THE CONTESTS

GET SHEET MUSIC OF
YOUR FAVOURITE
SINGERS. PRACTICE
SINGING AT HOME

ENTER
TALENT SHOWS

DEVELOP A COLLECTION
OF KARAOKE SONG
CATALOGUES AS SOUVENIRS

PURCHASE YOUR OWN
KARAOKE MACHINE – BUY KARAOKE
MUSIC AND USE IT TO
PRACTICE OR ENTERTAIN FRIENDS

PICK A STAGE
NAME AND
DEVELOP A STAGE
PRESENCE

Karaoke Singer

Broad Leisure Role

DEVELOP YOUR OWN
COLLECTION OF KARAOKE
TAPES AND LASER DISCS

PRACTICE THE SONGS
AND HOW YOU WILL
PERFORM THEM

BECOME A "RINGER" – SOMEONE
IN THE AUDIENCE THAT THE DJ
WILL CALL ON WHEN THINGS
NEED LIVENING UP

BUILD YOUR CONFIDENCE
IN SINGING AND AUDITION
FOR LOCAL MUSICAL
PRODUCTIONS

ENTER KARAOKE CONTESTS
AT BARS (LOCAL, MUNICIPAL,
PROVINCIAL, AND NATIONAL
LEVELS)

SING AT PRIVATE
PARTIES FOR
PART-TIME WORK

AUDITION FOR MUSICALS
– PERFORM ON STAGE

SING IN A BAND

DEVELOP FRIENDSHIPS
THAT CARRY OVER
TO OTHER PARTS OF
YOUR LIFE

TAKE VOICE LESSONS

JOIN A LOCAL
CHOIR OR
"GARAGE BAND"

WIN AND EXHIBIT
TROPHIES FROM
KARAOKE CONTESTS

FOLLOW THE KARAOKE DISC
JOCKEY FROM BAR TO BAR.
PARTICIPATE WITH OTHER
KARAOKE "REGULARS"

BECOME A KARAOKE
DISC JOCKEY

ENJOY THE EXCITEMENT
OF WONDERING, "WILL I
BE CALLED UP ON STAGE?"

ENJOY RAW TALENT
AND VOICES THAT HAVE
NOT BEEN PROFESSIONALLY
TRAINED

WEAR CLOTHES THAT
SUIT YOUR SINGING
REPERTOIRE (MADONNA
OR ELVIS LOOK ALIKE)

JOIN A TALENT AGENCY

BECOME A MEMBER
OF A FAN CLUB FOR YOUR
FAVOURITE PERFORMER

COMBINE INTEREST IN
SINGING WITH DANCING
AND ACTING

GET PICTURES OF
YOURSELF ON STAGE
AND COLLECT THEM
FOR A PHOTO ALBUM

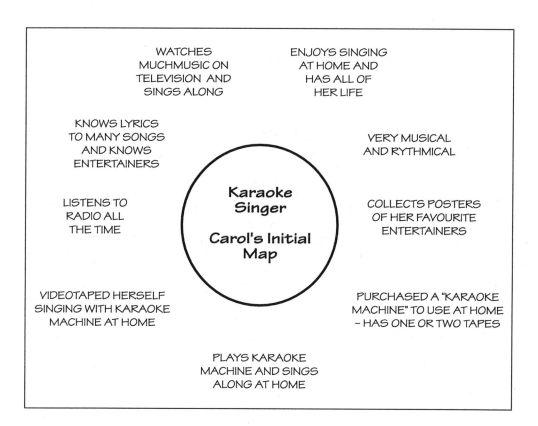

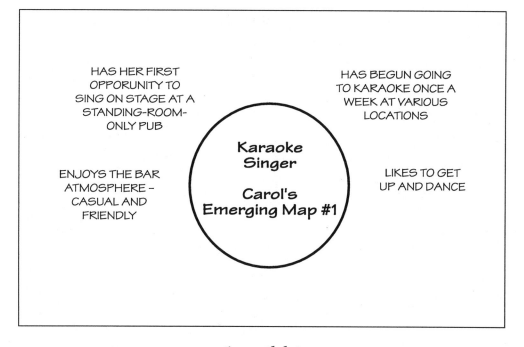

... 1 month later

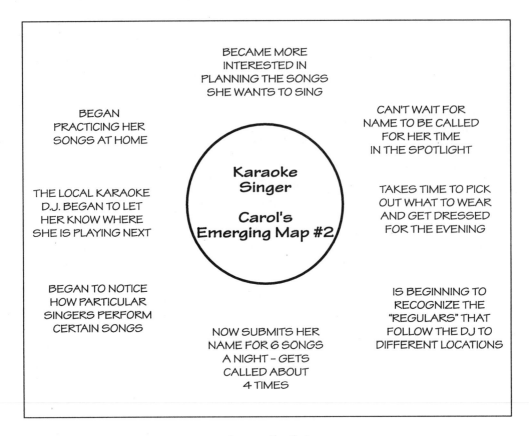

BECAME MORE
INTERESTED IN
PLANNING THE SONGS
SHE WANTS TO SING

BEGAN
PRACTICING HER
SONGS AT HOME

CAN'T WAIT FOR
NAME TO BE CALLED
FOR HER TIME
IN THE SPOTLIGHT

Karaoke
Singer

Carol's
Emerging Map #2

THE LOCAL KARAOKE
D.J. BEGAN TO LET
HER KNOW WHERE
SHE IS PLAYING NEXT

TAKES TIME TO PICK
OUT WHAT TO WEAR
AND GET DRESSED
FOR THE EVENING

BEGAN TO NOTICE
HOW PARTICULAR
SINGERS PERFORM
CERTAIN SONGS

IS BEGINNING TO
RECOGNIZE THE
"REGULARS" THAT
FOLLOW THE DJ TO
DIFFERENT LOCATIONS

NOW SUBMITS HER
NAME FOR 6 SONGS
A NIGHT – GETS
CALLED ABOUT
4 TIMES

... 4 months later

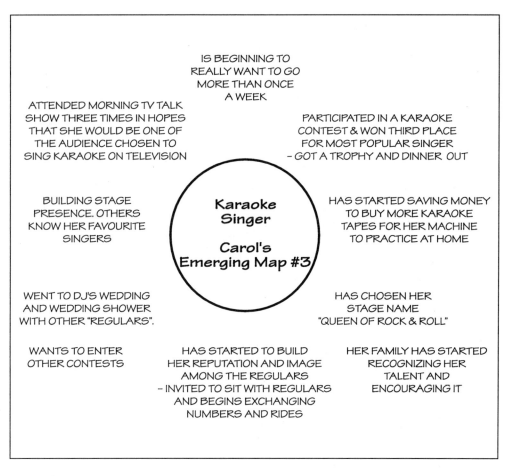

IS BEGINNING TO
REALLY WANT TO GO
MORE THAN ONCE
A WEEK

ATTENDED MORNING TV TALK
SHOW THREE TIMES IN HOPES
THAT SHE WOULD BE ONE OF
THE AUDIENCE CHOSEN TO
SING KARAOKE ON TELEVISION

PARTICIPATED IN A KARAOKE
CONTEST & WON THIRD PLACE
FOR MOST POPULAR SINGER
– GOT A TROPHY AND DINNER OUT

BUILDING STAGE
PRESENCE. OTHERS
KNOW HER FAVOURITE
SINGERS

Karaoke Singer

Carol's Emerging Map #3

HAS STARTED SAVING MONEY
TO BUY MORE KARAOKE
TAPES FOR HER MACHINE
TO PRACTICE AT HOME

WENT TO DJ'S WEDDING
AND WEDDING SHOWER
WITH OTHER "REGULARS".

HAS CHOSEN HER
STAGE NAME
"QUEEN OF ROCK & ROLL"

WANTS TO ENTER
OTHER CONTESTS

HAS STARTED TO BUILD
HER REPUTATION AND IMAGE
AMONG THE REGULARS
– INVITED TO SIT WITH REGULARS
AND BEGINS EXCHANGING
NUMBERS AND RIDES

HER FAMILY HAS STARTED
RECOGNIZING HER
TALENT AND
ENCOURAGING IT

... 8 months later

IS BUILDING HER
COLLECTION OF KARAOKE
TAPES FOR HER
KARAOKE MACHINE

HAS A STAGE NAME
"QUEEN OF ROCK & ROLL"

GOES TO KARAOKE
NIGHTS ONCE A
WEEK AT LOCAL PUBS

HAS A TROPHY FOR
MOST POPULAR
SINGER IN CONTEST

IS GETTING TO KNOW
OTHER "REGULARS"
SOCIALLY OUTSIDE
OF KARAOKE
EVENINGS

KEEPS EXPANDING
HER REPERTOIRE
OF SONGS AND
PERFORMERS

IS NOW BUYING
KARAOKE STAGE
CLOTHES

Karaoke Singer

Carol's Snapshot Identity Map

PRACTICES HER SONGS
AT HOME BEFORE
SHE GOES OUT

GETS DISAPPOINTED
WHEN HER NAME IS NOT
CALLED ENOUGH TO
APPEAR ON STAGE

MAKING MORE TAPES
OF HERSELF AT HOME

HER STAGE PRESENCE
IS IMPROVING

FRIENDS ARE CALLING
UP TO TAKE HER OUT
TO KARAOKE NIGHTS

IS STARTING TO KNOW
WHERE KARAOKE BARS
ARE IN HER COMMUNITY

IS DEVELOPING A
REPUTATION LOCALLY
AS A PASSIONATE SINGER

The Golfer

When you first meet Rick, it is obvious that he is a painfully quiet, withdrawn man who keeps very much to himself. He doesn't seem to get too excited about life and is remarkably steady in his demeanour. When staff first began getting to know his rhythm it was clear that his day was very orderly and structured. He was a man of habit and was comforted by routines. He works part-time as a computer technician, entering the provincial soccer scores onto computer. Rick seemed to want to do something that was quiet and low key.

When he said he was interested in becoming a golfer it seemed a natural choice. It is a gentleman's sport that has lots of contemplative aspects to it. It is not too flamboyant and it can be done at an even, quiet pace. When Rick had lived at home, his father had been somewhat of a golfer. Rick had never had the opportunity to learn golf from his father and so he wanted to learn now.

Rick began by taking two series of private lessons from a golf pro. This introduced him to the basics of the swing. At first, Rick could not keep up physically. It took him forever to hit one ball. He had to have everything perfect before he would swing. Bob, the golf Pro, enjoyed Rick's slow and determined approach to the game. Because Rick was far too withdrawn to say more than a couple of words to his Pro during his lessons, Bob decided to take him out for a beer to loosen him up. Bob and Rick went out to a local sports pub. To Bob's amazement his silent student was gifted at a computer game called Sports Trivia. Rick was widely versed in a number of sports and knew the dates of major events and the names of key celebrities. This became something the two of them could do together.

After the basic lessons, Rick agreed to play a round of golf on a public nine-hole golf course. He was extremely anxious about playing with others in a real game. He knew how slow he was in taking his swing and retrieving the balls that had gone off course. His first few experiences were less than positive. For one thing, course attendants kept coming around on the carts and asking them to let other foursomes play through or go ahead. On another occasion, while playing a game of golf, one of the players in Rick's foursome was hit in the eye with a stray ball. This accident was disturbing to Rick and left him unsure about how safe golfing was. It was awhile before he was willing to get back on a golf course again after that. By the time he did go back, he had decided that he would be better prepared for the time pressures.

Rick likes his daily routine to be predictable, and for that reason he found himself getting upset over having to cancel his plans for golf due to rain or inclement weather. This, along with the frustrations he was feeling from always being rushed on the golf course, led him to purchase a book of vouchers for an indoor driving range so that he could go more frequently and practise his swing. Rick enjoyed going regularly to the driving range because it allowed him to begin to recognize some of faces of the people and get to know another Pro. Gradually through practice, his upper body strength improved and so did his swing.

Rick was also interested in working on his putting. He began searching out mini-golf courses in and around Brampton. This was sheer enjoyment for Rick, especially on days where there were no lineups and lots of room to play. He began trying to find people who would come with him to play mini-golf. He wanted people who shared his enthusiasm. By going out frequently, Rick began to improve his putting.

It was very difficult throughout the project to get Rick to speak directly to staff. He rarely became animated about anything. When he did speak, it was in a monotone. When he was asked what he liked most about golf, however he sat straight up in his chair and said in a strong passionate voice "It's a relaxing game and you have fun with it. Playing golf makes me feel pretty good."

ENJOY BEING
OUT OF DOORS
WALKING

CAN READ
GOLFING MAGAZINES
AND BOOKS

STRONG ASPECT OF
INITIATION – GET ASKED
TO PLAY WITH BETTER
AND BETTER PLAYERS

TAKES A LOT OF
PRACTICE TO GO
BEYOND EACH
LEVEL OF PLAY

CAN PLAY IN GOLF
TOURNAMENTS
AMATEUR, SEMI-PRO
AND HOUSE LEAGUE

HIGH ANTICIPATION
FACTOR DUE TO
SEASONAL NATURE

LEARN THROUGH
IMITATING PEERS
AND PROS

Golfer
Broad Leisure Role

DEVELOP FRIENDSHIPS:
– INTIMATE
– ACQUAINTANCE

STATUS AND PRESTIGE
RELATED TO MEMBER-
SHIP AT GOLF CLUB

NEED TO LEARN
GENTLEMEN'S/
LADIES' ETIQUETTE

NEED TO BUY OR
RENT GOLF CLUBS

CLUB MEMBERSHIP
EXPANDS SOCIAL
NETWORK

SEEK OUT MINI-GOLF
AND PUTTING RANGES
– INDOOR AND OUTDOOR

CLUB MEMBERSHIP
CAN BE COSTLY

DRIVING RANGES
INDOOR/OUTDOOR

CAN FOLLOW THE
SUN – TRAVEL TO FIND
SUNNY GOLF COURSES

CAN PLAY AGAINST
YOUR OWN SCORE
– SELF IMPROVEMENT

CAN PLAY ON VIDEO
COMPUTER
SIMULATORS

SCORE KEEPING
HAS AN ASPECT
OF HONOUR

TECHNICAL GAME

CAN TAKE LESSONS
PRIVATE/PUBLIC

CAN FOLLOW PRO TOURS
– WATCH TOURNAMENTS
LIVE OR ON TV

"GOLF TALK"
EAGLES,
BIRDIES

STRONG ELEMENT
OF PACING ONESELF
AND STRATEGY

OFTEN HIGH
TIME INVESTMENT
– "GOLF WIDOW"

CAN BE TAKEN
UP BY COUPLES

SELF IMPROVEMENT
VIDEOS AND BOOKS
ABOUT GOLF

STRONG CONTEMPLATIVE
ASPECTS OF THE
GAME AND
CONCENTRATION

REQUIRES A CERTAIN
LOOK, STYLE – OFTEN
FORMAL RULES
ABOUT DRESS

CAN SPEND SOCIAL
TIME AFTER THE GAME
IN THE CLUBHOUSE
WITH FRIENDS

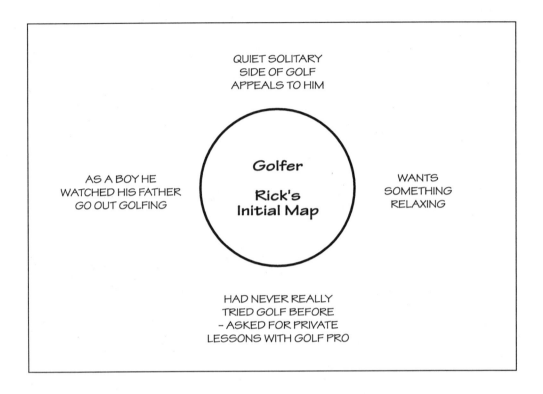

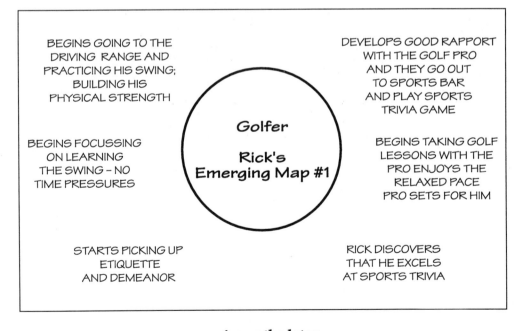

... 4 months later

GOES BACK TO DRIVING
RANGE TO PRACTICE MORE
– TRIES DIFFERENT
DRIVING RANGES

PLAYS HIS FIRST
ROUND OF GOLF
FEELS PRESSURED

SWING BEGINS TO
IMPROVE AND SO
DOES HIS SPEED

Golfer

**Rick's
Emerging Map #2**

BUYS HIS OWN
CLUBS. BEGINS
SHOPPING FOR
GOLF SHOES

STARTS ASKING TO
PLAY NINE HOLES
GOES WITH LEISURE
SUPPORT WORKER

BEGINS ASKING TO
GO TO MINI GOLF
TO PRACTICE PUTTING
– ENJOYS ATMOSPHERE

DECIDES HE LIKES INDOOR
DRIVING RANGES. DOESN'T
HAVE TO WORRY ABOUT
WEATHER CONDITIONS

... 6 months later

STARTS THINKING ABOUT
WHO HE WOULD LIKE
TO PLAY GOLF WITH

PASSIONATE, ANIMATED
TALKS FREELY ABOUT
HOW IT MAKES HIM
FEEL GOOD, HOW
RELAXING IT IS

FIGURES OUT WHO ELSE
DESCRIBES HIMSELF
AS A GOLFER

SPEED AND
STRENGTH
IMPROVING

Golfer

**Rick's
Emerging Map #3**

WANTS TO
BUY HIS
OWN PUTTERS

BEGINS LEARNING
THE GOLF
RULE BOOK

FEELS ANTICIPATION –
WAITING FOR
SUMMER GOLFING

TALKS ABOUT BUYING
GOLF SHOES

BUYS DISCOUNT TICKETS
FOR DRIVING RANGE
SO HE CAN AFFORD TO
GO MORE FREQUENTLY

STARTS DIFFERENTIATING
CLUBS BEFORE HE
USES THEM – BEGINS
PLAYING MINI GOLF

HIS GIRLFRIEND ESTER
SEES GOLF AS
A WAY THEY MIGHT
CONNECT – BEGINS
TAKING LESSONS

... 10 months later

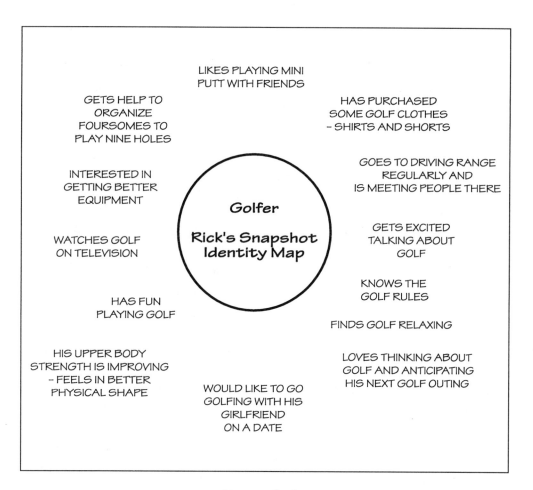

... 12 months later

The Karate Student

When you first meet Andy you are confronted by his downward gaze. He seems to wear his oppression round about his shoulders. The weight of his life experiences are forcing him to look like a young man already defeated. Contradicting this image, is a shock of bright red hair that signifies that side of him that is ready to take you on at any moment. When staff first approached Andy about what he might like to do in his leisure, he had two very clear messages. First, he wanted to get out of his family's home into a place of his own and second, he wanted to be able to have a friend over once in a while. Relationships with people his age were very important to him. Aside from his brother who had just left home, he had no real friends to hang out with. Staff began supporting him to get together with his friends more and worked with his family to improve the situation at home.

Andy was not happy when we first met him. He was getting into scraps and fights with people at the shopping mall. He is not a big man. He is, in fact, quite small in stature. His second-hand clothes dwarfed him because they were always two or three sizes too big and had to be rolled up at the sleeves and hem. From our discussions with Andy, it seemed that he might be interested in some form of martial arts. When asked if he would be interested Andy was rather tentative at first. He was not familiar with martial arts. We took him to the local gym to see for himself. It was that first visit to the local karate club that marked the beginning of Andy's metamorphosis. The deliberateness and the discipline of the art of karate was something that attracted him. He signed up right away at the local Karate club for private lessons two nights a week.

The first requirement of membership was to purchase an all-white *guy* (Japanese for "uniform"). When members arrived at the club they removed their outdoor shoes and went into the change room to put on their *guys*. Andy treated his *guy* with the utmost of reverence. When he put it on he was transformed. He smiled from ear to ear.

In his first few classes Andy was taught all of the ritualistic gestures and phrases necessary before one enters the *DoJo* (Japanese for "gym") and before entering into mock combat with other members. Andy seemed to find these disciplines very appealing and took pride in his ability to remember them.

The lessons involved a combination of physical conditioning and learning several defence postures and moves. Andy had one instructor named Doug. This relationship proved to be invaluable for introducing him to other members of the club. Doug treated Andy with a lot of respect, which put Andy at ease. Andy imitated the confident strong movements of his instructor, and throughout the lessons it was remarkable to see the physical transformation in him. His body seemed to bristle with the excitement of his new-found passion. While he was in his *guy* and even when he was on his way to the gym, he began to stand taller and walk with his head held high.

Karate became the centre of Andy's week. He could not wait to get to the gym for his next lesson. He was animated whenever he talked about karate, what he knew and what he was learning. After several months, it became clear that Andy needed gym clothes to attend the club. He was arriving at the gym in ill-fitting street clothes while everyone else wore track suits and running shoes. Andy bought some athletic clothes and a gym bag. This made a tremendous difference in his willingness to walk into the gym and begin talking to other club members. It was obvious that before, his energy had been taken up in getting his shoes off and getting changed into his *guy* as soon as possible so that he would feel more like he belonged.

It wasn't long before Andy began participating in the social fabric of the club by attending the Saturday *Do Jo* clean up parties. This led to his becoming part of a small volunteer group that met every Tuesday morning at the gym to do chores or cleaning assignments given by the *Sensai* or Master Instructor. At Christmas, staff went out with Andy to buy a suit so that he could attend the Club Christmas party. This was an experience to be remembered. Andy danced all night with club members and socialized with people to whom Doug had introduced him.

Being a Karate student has helped Andy to be more sure of himself and more assertive in all areas of his life. His sense of self has changed and he is now far less likely to be wandering the streets or the mall for something to do. He has found a place to belong—the local karate club.

LEARN ABOUT
MEDITATION AND
CONCENTRATION

HELPS TO DEVELOP
ASSERTIVENESS
AND SELF AWARENESS

CAN FEEL THE
ENERGY RISING
FROM THE GROUP
— EVERYONE MOVES
IN SYNC AND BECOMES
AS ONE PERSON

CLUB PARTIES
THROUGHOUT
THE YEAR —
SOCIALIZE BEFORE
AND AFTER

MEMBERSHIP
INVOLVES CERTAIN
RESPONSIBILITIES —
PARTICIPATE IN CLUB
ROLES, CLEAN UP, ETC.

Karate Kai

**Broad
Leisure Role**

WORK IN TEAMS —
LEARN LEADERSHIP
BY ROTATING
CAPTAINS

CAN TAKE UP
OTHER MARTIAL ARTS
AND MEDITATIVE
PRACTICES

CAN JOIN THE CLUB
— BE A MEMBER OR
TAKE PRIVATE
LESSONS

BUILD CONFIDENCE
IN KNOWING THAT
YOU CAN PROTECT
YOURSELF

EXPECTED TO
TAKE IT SERIOUSLY
AND PRACTICE

CAN MAKE YOU
INTERESTED IN
SPIRITUAL PURSUITS

TEACHES A
WAY OF LIFE

PERIODIC RANKING
AND TESTING — GROUP
CELEBRATES ACHIEVEMENTS
WITH YOU — SO YOU
TRY YOUR BEST

INVOLVES MENTAL
AND PHYSICAL
CONDITIONING

CLUB MEMBERSHIP
IS AFFORDABLE
($40—$60/MONTH)

DISPLAY BELT COLOURS
AS TROPHIES AND
STATUS SYMBOLS

LEARN TO RESPECT
OTHERS — ACCEPT
PEOPLE AS THEY ARE

SKILL PROGRESSION
AT EACH BELT LEVEL

EVERYONE WEARS
THE SAME UNIFORM

LEARN SELF-DISCIPLINE
— CONTROL OF TEMPER

LEARN JAPANESE
WORDS AND PHRASES

GETS INTO
TROUBLE
BECAUSE HE IS
SO ANGRY

DOESN'T FEEL
GOOD ABOUT
HIMSELF – WANTS
TO GET INTO SHAPE

Karate Kai

**Andy's
Initial Map**

SHOWS AN
INTEREST IN
LEARNING TO
PROTECT HIMSELF

WILLING TO FIND
OUT WHAT KARATE
IS ALL ABOUT

VISITS THE CLUB
– LIKES THE
ATMOSPHERE
IMMEDIATELY

WAITS FOR NEXT
LESSON WITH HIGH
ANTICIPATION

LOVES LEARNING
JAPANESE WORDS
AND CUSTOMS

BUYS A "GUY" AND
CAN'T WAIT TO GET
IT ON WHEN HE
ARRIVES AT THE CLUB

Karate Kai

**Andy's
Emerging Map #1**

BEGINS PRIVATE
KARATE LESSONS –
LOVES THE ATTENTION
OF THE INSTRUCTOR

GETS A RIDE TO
AND FROM THE GYM
TWICE A WEEK

BEGINS TO CATCH
ON TO THE MOVES –
SLOWLY AT FIRST

STARTS SAYING
"HELLO" TO MEMBERS
OF THE CLUB BEFORE
AND AFTER LESSONS

CLEARLY NEEDS TO
WORK ON HIS PHYSICAL
FITNESS – ESPECIALLY
ENDURANCE AND FLEXIBILITY

HAS TROUBLE REMEMBERING
THE MOVES BETWEEN
CLASSES – STARTS COMING
BACK TO HIM DURING
THE LESSON

... 1 month later

CONTINUES WITH
LESSONS TWICE A WEEK
– ENJOYS HIS RELATIONSHIP
WITH THE INSTRUCTOR

SHOWS OBVIOUS CHANGES
IN HIS SELF CONCEPT AND
BODY AWARENESS –
WALKS TALLER AND IS
MORE CONFIDENT

Karate Kai

**Andy's
Emerging Map #2**

STARTS BEING CONSCIOUS
OF THE NEED FOR PROPER
GYM CLOTHES – BUYS A GYM
BAG AND TRACK SUIT

IS INVITED TO COME TO
THE GYM ON A SATURDAY
TO CLEAN IT UP WITH
CLUB MEMBERS – MEETS
OTHER MEMBERS

STARTS TELLING
PEOPLE HE KNOWS
WHAT HE IS DOING –
REALLY ENTHUSIASTIC

BEGINS ASKING ABOUT
MEMBERSHIP – UNCERTAIN
IF HE WANTS GROUP LESSONS
– ENJOYS THE
ONE-ON-ONE LESSONS

INSTRUCTOR ENCOURAGES HIM
TO COME TO THE CHRISTMAS
PARTY – ANDY GOES AND ENJOYS
MEETING OTHER PEOPLE

WANTS TO BE AT THE GYM
AT OTHER TIMES – APPROACHED
ABOUT VOLUNTEERING EVERY
TUESDAY WITH OTHER
MEMBERS – HE BEGINS TO VOLUNTEER

INSTRUCTOR SOMETIMES
DRIVES HIM HOME
AFTER CLASS

... 5 months later

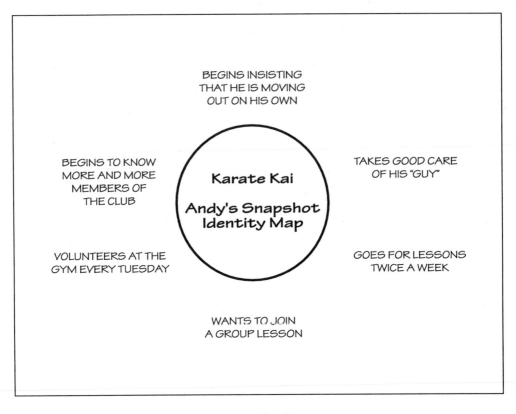

BEGINS INSISTING
THAT HE IS MOVING
OUT ON HIS OWN

BEGINS TO KNOW
MORE AND MORE
MEMBERS OF
THE CLUB

Karate Kai

**Andy's Snapshot
Identity Map**

TAKES GOOD CARE
OF HIS "GUY"

VOLUNTEERS AT THE
GYM EVERY TUESDAY

GOES FOR LESSONS
TWICE A WEEK

WANTS TO JOIN
A GROUP LESSON

... 8 months later

The Private Fitness Club Member

Sean is in constant motion. He seems to experience the world through his hands. So much of how he comes to know things is by touching them and gaining a "feel" for how they work. He loves to run, full out, especially when he is running alongside someone else. His cardiovascular system is in great shape. All of these things led us to believe that he enjoyed keeping himself in shape and doing fitness activities.

Sean communicates in several different ways. He can tell you what he wants by physically taking you by the hand and pointing out the object of his desire. He can, when he chooses to, speak in a soft almost indiscernible whisper. He can also speak by spelling words out on a computer keypad or simply by the way his behaviors communicate his happiness and/or his anger and discontent.

Staff began dreaming with Sean by taking him places and observing his reactions. It takes him a while to become familiar with a place. He is constantly investigating it. If it is somewhere he really doesn't like he will let you know right away. It is not quite that easy for places he likes. He seems to need a lot of time to make a decision about a place, to check it out.

In visiting fitness clubs, Sean was very clear about which ones he disliked. Those clubs that were exclusive and rather unfriendly were ruled out quickly. Staff knew he had settled on a particular fitness club, the day he began showing that he did not want to leave when it was time to go. There was so much to do, so many novel pieces of equipment and so many new faces. This fitness club appealed to Sean because there were not a lot of people together at any one time and he could deal with people on a one to one basis.

It was obvious that Sean enjoyed and benefited from having a regular routine. Once he became a member of the club he went two or three times a week. The familiar rhythm seemed to calm him because he knew pretty much what to expect. It wasn't long before he had settled on a work-out routine that he could carry out each visit.

Fairly early in his involvement in the club, Sean began making it clear to his support worker that he wanted to look like him and the others in the gym. He began to closely follow and mimic the style of his dress. If the support worker tucked in his T-shirt and rolled up his sleeves, so did Sean. If he left his T-shirt hanging out over his track pants Sean would quickly follow suit. He was also very proud of his membership card and carried it into each part of the club at all times.

Over time, Sean overcame his fascination with standing back and observing the up and down movement of the weight equipment and took an interest in learning how to use them for weight training. He wasn't the least bit interested in the standard three-part instruction series given by the fitness staff. He was keen to get started right away by imitating what he had seen other club members doing. It was remarkable how much he had taken in from his observer stance.

Initially, Sean did not seem to want to do a full "work out" on the fitness equipment. His interest was roused only once he realized that strengthening his body would help him run faster. Running faster appeared to be a primary motivation for Sean. He felt good when he ran. So good in fact, it was difficult to slow him down on the indoor track. While others settled into a slower jogging pace, Sean would sprint around the track until he had exhausted himself.

The indoor track and the outdoor pool were probably Sean's favorite parts of the club. Both areas of the club, however, had rules that were at first difficult for him to get used to. Members were expected to stay in the lanes while using both the pool and the indoor track. So as not to interfere with the training of other club members. This was a matter of etiquette at the club. Sean came to the club so full of energy that disciplining his workout into laps and lanes was not easy. He was not interested in simply jogging around the track. After a few months, Sean had found a happy medium to his sprinting around the track. He began power striding, that is walking quickly with large bold steps. In addition, he and his support worker began figuring out ways for Sean to have opportunities for running full out like the wind, both on his own and with others.

MAY NEED SPECIALIZED
EQUIPMENT – LIKE A
SQUASH RACQUET

MAY HAVE A FAMILY
FITNESS ATMOSPHERE
– "SOMETHING FOR
EVERYONE"

PROVIDES A SOCIAL NETWORK
– MAY BE A PLACE FOR
YOUNG PROFESSIONALS
TO FIND BUSINESS CONTACTS
OR TO MAKE FRIENDS

STATUS AND PRESTIGE
ASSOCIATED WITH
MEMBERSHIP

OFTEN PEOPLE SIGN
UP WITH A FRIEND WITH THE
INTENT TO GO TOGETHER

MAY BE CLUBS WITHIN
THE CLUB: JOGGING CLUB

**Fitness Club
Member**

**Broad
Leisure Role**

STRONG INTEREST IN
BODY IMAGE AND BODY
AWARENESS

PUBLIC OR PRIVATE
CLUBS – GENERALIZED
OR SPECIALIZED
MEMBERSHIP

SEMI-COMPETITIVE
LEAGUES SO YOU
HAVE PEOPLE TO
PLAY AGAINST

SET UP FOR "SERIOUS
ATHLETES" TRAINING
FOR PARTICIPATION IN
AMATEUR SPORTS

HEALTH CONSCIOUS
ATTITUDE
OF MEMBERS

MAY HAVE INFORMAL
LADDERS SET UP FOR PLAY
AMONG MEMBERS –
ESPECIALLY IN
RACQUET SPORTS

LEARN ABOUT
PERSONAL HEALTH
AND FITNESS

MAY HAVE ROOMS TO
RENT FOR
PRIVATE PARTIES

MAY HAVE SPORTS BARS
INCORPORATED
INTO THE CLUB

MAY HAVE A "SPA"
ATMOSPHERE AND
INCLUDE SERVICES LIKE
HYDROTHERAPY, MASSAGE,
AROMATHERAPY,
ACUPUNCTURE,
REFLEXOLOGY,
CHIROPRACTIC,
NUTRITIONAL
COUNSELLING ...

MAY HOLD WORKSHOPS
ON FITNESS-RELATED
TOPICS – SKILL COURSES

CAN USE THE CLUB
NON- COMPETITIVELY

LEARN HOW TO DESIGN
PERSONAL TRAINING
ROUTINES

MAY HAVE A GIFT STORE
WITH FITNESS BOOKS,
EQUIPMENT AND
PARAPHERNALIA

LEARN ABOUT WEIGHT
AND CARDIOVASCULAR
MACHINES – HOW TO USE
THEM FOR MAXIMUM EFFECT

"SINGLES CULTURE" – EVENTS
ORGANIZED TO CREATE
OPPORTUNITIES FOR MEN
AND WOMEN TO MEET

CASUAL PLACES IN CLUB
TO MEET FOR MEALS OR
HEALTHY SNACKS – BEFORE
OR AFTER THE GAME

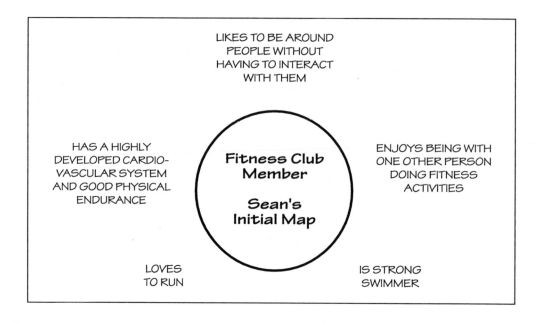

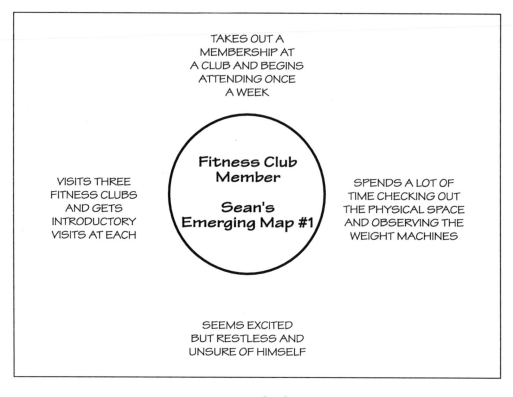

... 2 months later

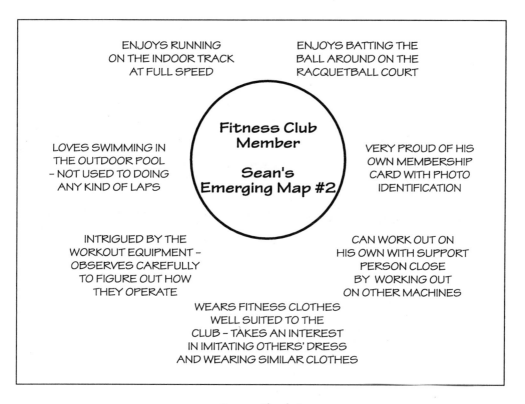

... 3 months later

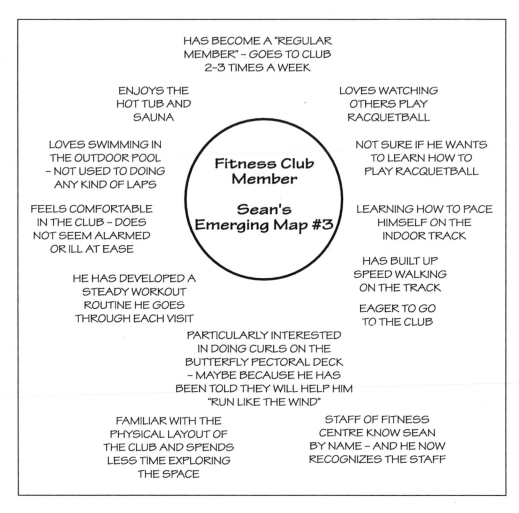

HAS BECOME A "REGULAR
MEMBER" – GOES TO CLUB
2–3 TIMES A WEEK

ENJOYS THE
HOT TUB AND
SAUNA

LOVES WATCHING
OTHERS PLAY
RACQUETBALL

LOVES SWIMMING IN
THE OUTDOOR POOL
– NOT USED TO DOING
ANY KIND OF LAPS

**Fitness Club
Member**

**Sean's
Emerging Map #3**

NOT SURE IF HE WANTS
TO LEARN HOW TO
PLAY RACQUETBALL

FEELS COMFORTABLE
IN THE CLUB – DOES
NOT SEEM ALARMED
OR ILL AT EASE

LEARNING HOW TO PACE
HIMSELF ON THE
INDOOR TRACK

HAS BUILT UP
SPEED WALKING
ON THE TRACK

HE HAS DEVELOPED A
STEADY WORKOUT
ROUTINE HE GOES
THROUGH EACH VISIT

EAGER TO GO
TO THE CLUB

PARTICULARLY INTERESTED
IN DOING CURLS ON THE
BUTTERFLY PECTORAL DECK
– MAYBE BECAUSE HE HAS
BEEN TOLD THEY WILL HELP HIM
"RUN LIKE THE WIND"

FAMILIAR WITH THE
PHYSICAL LAYOUT OF
THE CLUB AND SPENDS
LESS TIME EXPLORING
THE SPACE

STAFF OF FITNESS
CENTRE KNOW SEAN
BY NAME – AND HE NOW
RECOGNIZES THE STAFF

... 5 months later

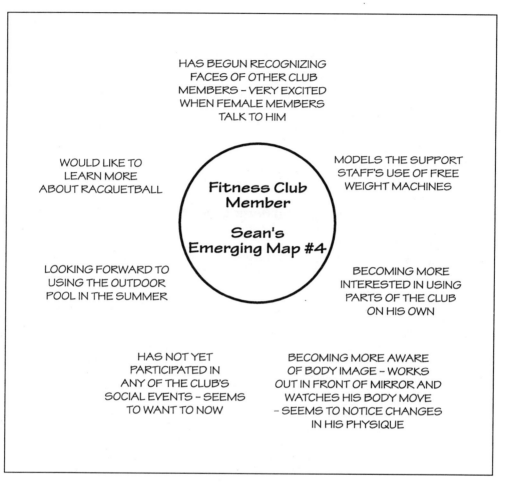

HAS BEGUN RECOGNIZING
FACES OF OTHER CLUB
MEMBERS – VERY EXCITED
WHEN FEMALE MEMBERS
TALK TO HIM

WOULD LIKE TO
LEARN MORE
ABOUT RACQUETBALL

**Fitness Club
Member**

**Sean's
Emerging Map #4**

MODELS THE SUPPORT
STAFF'S USE OF FREE
WEIGHT MACHINES

LOOKING FORWARD TO
USING THE OUTDOOR
POOL IN THE SUMMER

BECOMING MORE
INTERESTED IN USING
PARTS OF THE CLUB
ON HIS OWN

HAS NOT YET
PARTICIPATED IN
ANY OF THE CLUB'S
SOCIAL EVENTS – SEEMS
TO WANT TO NOW

BECOMING MORE AWARE
OF BODY IMAGE – WORKS
OUT IN FRONT OF MIRROR AND
WATCHES HIS BODY MOVE
– SEEMS TO NOTICE CHANGES
IN HIS PHYSIQUE

... 9 months later

HAS A REGULAR FITNESS
ROUTINE AND WORKOUT –
USES A LOT OF DIFFERENT
EQUIPMENT AND
ENJOYS THEM ALL

GRADUALLY
LEARNING THE
"RULES" OF THE CLUB
AND CLUB ETIQUETTE

WANTS TO
LOOK INTO A
RUNNING CLUB

LIKES BEING AROUND
AND MEETING
WOMEN MEMBERS

WOULD LIKE TO GO
TO ONE OF THE
SOCIAL EVENTS

**Fitness Club
Member**

**Snapshot
Identity Map**

HAS A NUMBER OF
FITNESS OUTFITS TO
WEAR FOR WORKOUTS
AT THE CLUB

BECOMING QUITE
FASHION CONSCIOUS
– WANTS TO LOOK
THE PART

ENJOYS THE STATUS
OF CLUB
MEMBERSHIP – PROUD
OF HIS MEMBERSHIP CARD

LIKES TO GO TO
THE CLUB ON A REGULAR
BASIS – AT LEAST
ONCE OR TWICE A WEEK

KNOWS THE CLUB STAFF
BY NAME – STARTING TO
RECOGNIZE AND TALK TO
OTHER REGULAR MEMBERS

BEGINNING TO TAKE A
REAL INTEREST IN HIS
BODY SHAPE AND TONE
– FEELING STRONGER
AND LOOKING STRONGER

BECOMING LESS AGITATED
AT HOME BECAUSE HE KNOWS
HE CAN WORKOUT AT THE
GYM AND USE UP SOME OF
HIS EXTRA ENERGY

... 12 months later

Major Learnings

The key insights and learnings that arose out of the project have widespread or even universal applicability. They will be helpful in a whole range of leisure and human service settings, and to individuals with disabilities and their families as they begin to address more fully the realm of leisure.

Table Six
Major Learnings

1) Leisure as event, diversion or treat

2) People's dreams fundamentally involve relationship-building

3) Motives and meanings are many and varied

4) People's choices are affected by other's ignorances and prejudices

5) Developing leisure identities involves a strong perception of risk

6) Development of each person's leisure identity has its own natural rhythm and learning curve

7) People tend to learn skills related to their passions at a more accelerated rate than usual

8) Providing support to maintain a leisure identity is as important as supporting its development

9) Relationships with connectors and people who are part of the "associational" life of the community must be fostered

10) Overriding concerns must be dealt with

---

1) Leisure as Event, Diversion or Treat

People with disabilities, and especially those who have been involved with human services, tend to have an activity or "event" orientation to leisure. It is something they experience as a series of discrete events in their lives. They are typically not accustomed to sticking with a particular leisure interest over a long time or being supported to incorporate the interest into their overall life.

There may be a number of factors involved. Due to not having many friends, people with disabilities spend their leisure time with human service staff or family members who tend to "take them along" to leisure events they are going to, whenever they can. As a result, leisure tends to be sporadic, infrequent and unreliable. Individuals cannot typically count on it for building any continuity of experience or relationship base. It also does not reflect anything of themselves, who they are and what they like because it is not necessarily something they would have chosen.

In addition, many individuals with disabilities have a sparse social network. They have few relationships which act as models for leisure identity development. They also have few people in their lives who act as "guides" into the complex associational fabric of the community, so they do not know where to begin to find people who share the same kind of interest or passion. Leisure-related clubs and associations are difficult to access without having someone to make the initial introductions and provide ongoing support of some kind.

The discontinuity of the human service system is also a contributing factor. Staff come and go out of their lives. Once an interest or passion is identified or even taken up it is not maintained.

Along with this "event" orientation, the most common experiences of leisure for persons with disabilities, have typically been purely exploratory. They have been expected to try this and that with no intention or belief that they may really want to or be capable of pursuing anything as a serious interest.

As well, leisure is presented as a diversion, as something that parents and staff do to "entertain" the individual, to "keep them busy," to divert them from the monotony of their lives – with little expectation of it holding meaning in and of itself.

Leisure may also be viewed as a "treat" – something given as a reward for good behavior rather than a personal need or right. Or it is viewed as "respite" – time for the family or caregiver to take a break from caring for the individual.

These experiences and perceptions of leisure presented obstacles throughout the project. They were especially entrenched in individuals who had spent long periods of their lives in human services. As individuals were supported to follow their dreams, and they began to feel the benefits of participation, these perceptions began to transform very gradually.

2) People's Dreams Fundamentally Involve Relationship-Building

When people were asked about what they most wanted in their leisure they often described it in terms of relationships. "I want to be able to go dancing with my boyfriend. I want us to have fun together and laugh." When people can get support to build, strengthen, maintain or re-establish significant relationships in their lives while engaging in leisure, they become more able to focus on defining their specific leisure interests. As well, leisure contexts support the development of social networks and provide a unique opportunity for building intimacy. Intimacy is essential to all of us. Two stories illustrate the need to view relationship-building as key to providing support to people in their leisure.

Bill and Bernice

Bernice sat across from me at the restaurant looking terribly shy and yet letting me know that there was so much to know about her, so much she wanted to explain. She blushed deep red as she described her dreams and what she had always wanted to do with her life. It took awhile until she came around to what she thought we could help her with the most. Once she spoke of Bill, her ex-boyfriend, her face lit up and radiated hope. Above all else she wanted us to help her reunite with Bill. When we explored with her how the relationship had come to an end and what could be done now to re-establish it she became very distraught. The relationship had meant so much to her, yet it seemed to have vanished the same way other relationships in her life had. At the crux of the problem between Bill and Bernice was the fact that they could not communicate very effectively with one another. Bill was deaf and used sign language and gesturing to make himself understood. Bernice did not know any sign language. What aggravated things was that Bill would try to finger spell or print out certain words to her and she was unable to figure out the meanings, because she had never learned to read or write. Around the end of their relationship the interaction between them had become very strained and even hostile.

We decided to begin by helping Bill and Bernice find a method of communicating so that they could make some decisions about their relationship. Our initial efforts focussed on ensuring that they both felt safe being together again. It was important that they both discover that they were capable of having a more positive, loving interaction. We began taking them on double dates to restaurants, to live theatre and to billiard halls.

Martha, a woman with a lot of expertise in developing alternative methods of communication, began helping us find a way for the couple to communicate. This involved having Bernice and Bill talk about what they had always wanted to tell each other. These words and concepts were used as their initial vocabulary for communicating. They were made into pictures or symbols that both of them understood. The pictures were put into a leather portfolio that Bernice could easily carry around with her. Under the picture was the actual word or phrase so that as they pointed to the symbols Bernice would begin associating the written word with the picture and the meaning. This new-found communication potential had a remarkable impact on Bill and Bernice. Bernice's whole demeanour seemed to change. She was noticeably less agitated, and more serene in Bill's presence. She was more able to get across her feelings. There was now hope for the two of them. They could get on with actually doing things together. Bill grinned from ear to ear when they were together. They quickly began to make plans together.

Once the relationship was stabilized, Bernice took more of an interest in herself and what she wanted to pursue on her own. She was no longer preoccupied with resolving her relationship. She now felt that she was able to invest time into one of her passions, which was not only attending fitness classes, but actually becoming a member of a fitness club. Bernice toured a number of fitness clubs and seemed most happy with the local Y.W.C.A. that was close by and with which she was already familiar. When she became a member, she began by participating in step aerobics classes. After a while, she started also going swimming regularly and attending a women's discussion group. What she likes most about her membership is the flexibility it gives her to take part in a range of things that are constantly being offered at the club. She also enjoys feeling that she knows the place and can go whenever she wants, after work and on weekends. It gives her a place to belong and something to do on her own when she is not with Bill.

Karen and Gerald

Karen and Gerald have lived together now for 2 years. Karen works part-time at McDonalds and until just recently Gerald worked at an auto auction. I knew Karen by her strong reputation as an outspoken self-advocate. It was clear that something was on her mind when she seemed unable to focus on talking about her own leisure the first night we met. As we tried to get Gerald talking it was clear that he also had another agenda. She and Gerald wanted to be married. They wanted it more than anything else in the world. Every conversation ended with the same question, what are you going to do to help us get married?

The decision to get married had been a liberating one for them both. They both had a strong conviction that it was "the right thing to do." It was what they wanted even if their families disagreed. They had been saving every last cent they had for their wedding and wanted it to be an unforgettable evening.

Karen was unsure of what was involved in organizing a wedding. She needed advice and was asking us to assist her in writing up lists of all the things she would need to do. There was no doubt that helping them both to get their wedding plans in place was their first priority.

Helping to plan the wedding involved discussions about how getting married might affect their Family Benefit cheques; where they might hold the wedding; who they would invite; how much the wedding cake would cost; what to write on the wedding invitations; how much it would cost to rent the hall and hire the minister; where to get a nice suit and wedding dress and how to get support from their families.

Once they had exchanged engagement rings, the hall and the minister had been booked and plans were underway, Karen and Gerald began talking more about other aspects of their lives. As with all newly engaged couples the dreams they had for their leisure involved things they could do together. They were quick to explain how big a fan they were of country and western line dancing. They talked about watching it on television and imagining themselves in full country and western dress dancing in rhythm together. As they described their dream, a strange feeling came over me. I could see Gerald with a ten gallon hat, western boots and an intricately embroidered shirt. He was a natural. It was as if he had stepped out of a western movie. It was obvious from the very beginning that they would both really enjoy going after this shared passion.

We began our support by helping them find out where the country and western bars were in town and when they had line dancing. Once we knew that, we began double dating and going there on nights when there was dancing. They loved it. You could tell they knew some of the moves even though they hadn't tried them on the dance floor themselves. They were eager to start private lessons.

Their lessons gave them the confidence they needed to nudge their way onto the dance floor. The western shirts and cowboy boots helped them feel they belonged. However, it was the excitement in their eyes as they completed their first line dance together, surrounded by several other couples that revealed their passion for their new identity.

3)   Motives and Meanings are Many and Varied

We all have a unique constellation of interests and passions. In the area of leisure, each of us has different motives for wanting to pursue our particular passions. These may change over time as our life situations change. Many of us find we are attracted to a certain passion or leisure identity without really knowing why we are so drawn to it, what deep meaning or significance it plays in our life. Taking a conscious inventory of what it has meant to us, what it has offered, can be very worthwhile. Individual differences in motivation and meaning need to be recognized and understood, in order to provide more effective support.

> *One needs something to believe in, something for which one can have*
> *wholehearted enthusiasm. One needs to feel that one's life has*
> *meaning, that one is needed in this world.*
>
> Hannah Senesh

Table Seven
Leisure Motives and Meanings

1. To gain a sense of belonging and/or membership and develop roots in the community.
2. To build or maintain relationships.
3. To enjoy yourself and find pleasure in life.
4. To escape from daily stresses and/or to relieve the pressure of routine.
5. To keep in shape and/or to develop physical stamina.
6. To learn about yourself.
7. To find something to do that is affordable and convenient as well as satisfying.
8. To find diversion from every day life and boredom.
9. To push the limits of your physical, emotional, spiritual, intellectual self.
10. To find thrill and adventure.
11. To feel connected and at one with nature.
12. To feel at peace with yourself and/or to develop spiritually.
13. To feel courageous.
14. To re-engage the playful side of yourself, laugh, be silly, find humour in life.
15. To feel a sense of accomplishment, gratification, achievement.
16. To recapture cherished memories of childhood.
17. To re-establish leisure identities that played a significant role in defining "who you were" as you were growing up.
18. To express those parts of you that go unexpressed in other more serious and more structured contexts.
19. To use the skills and competencies you have developed in work and family role contexts.
20. To hold on to self-perceptions you have of yourself as youthful and vital.
21. To find something that is compatible with family and work careers and to create a lifestyle that offers a sense of balance.
22. To find something that can be done within the family context to build family connections and strength.
23. To discover entirely new skill sets and competencies that are not part of your work or family roles.
24. To experiment with the way others perceive you and the way you perceive yourself.
25. To provide a sense of status, reputation and even prestige among peers and community.
26. To maintain an intergenerational tradition or skill, such as quilting, that was passed on to you by your grandmother.

Do nothing because it is righteous or praiseworthy or noble to do so;
do nothing because it seems good to do so; do only that which you
must do and which you cannot do in any other way.

Ursula K. Le Guin

The story below illustrates the need to keep listening to the person for indications of what really motivates his or her involvement or what meaning it has for them:

> Pauline is an avid soap opera fan. She can fill you in on who is dating whom and which star is playing what role. She seems most attracted to the glamour, the beautiful wardrobes and the sense of invincibility that the stars all portray. At times she appears almost caught up in the soap opera dramas she watches on television. Her dream was to star in a soap opera.

> When she was asked if she wanted to be part of a soap opera fan club she said no. She did ask once, however, if someone would go with her to see the stars of one of her shows at one of their autograph-signing appearances at a Toronto mall. She seemed to want the lifestyle of the rich and famous. She said she wanted to be on stage.

> Once we began exploring her dream with her it seemed she might be interested in acting in one of the local amateur theatres. After taking her to watch the audition nights at the local amateur theatres, she was certain that it was not really the acting she was interested in. We explored the idea of helping with props or costumes. She was not interested. She was drawn to the fantasy of bright lights and cameras.

> After a while she asked us to take out her out to watch some of the local theatre productions in Brampton. These productions seemed to leave her unenthused. They involved a lot of careful listening and attention. This is not easy for her. She wears hearing aids in both her ears and at times found it impossible to follow the dialogue.

> It finally became apparent to her and to us that she was most interested in the showbiz kinds of productions where you make it into a real evening out. She thoroughly enjoyed taking time to get dressed up and fix her beautiful red hair for dinner and a show. Not just any show either – it had to be a musical with lots of high energy dance routines and songs that she can recognize and sing along with. Over time, Pauline decided she liked Dinner Theatre best. Dinner Theatre is more interactive. The actors bring the show to you as you sit in your seats. Pauline comes alive as the actors come off the stage and "work the audience." This gives her a sense of being in contact with the stars and makes the evening have a special glow.

4) People's Choices are Affected by Other's Ignorances and Prejudices

We all tend to start our problem solving process with those solutions that seem the most plausible, the most do-able, the most familiar. This is also true during the dreaming process. We start with the familiar, or what is, rather than what could be. We do this not only when we are articulating dreams for ourselves, but also when we are supporting others to formulate their dreams. But the essense of dreaming is to go beyond describing what is, and look to the future. Only in that way do we expand our field of reference dramatically.

At those times when individuals seem stumped, and do not give any real suggestions about what they would like to pursue in their leisure, we must be able to listen carefully for any indication through speech or behavior about where to begin. We must be careful not to start with suggestions that reflect the passions of family members and/or support workers. When we inject our interests into a dreaming process we limit the person to our imaginations. We then severely hinder the individual from developing an imagination about his or her own possibilities and tuning in to what lights him or her up.

When individuals are stumped and are not giving any suggestions, what may be needed is more time for the individual to find a way to express her desires and to build her trust in the process. By taking time to explore various leisure experiences the individual can develop her preferences more and begin to zero in on her desires and passions. It may also be necessary to find better ways of determining the person's passions through observing her behaviors and leisure patterns, especially if she does not express herself verbally.

We can all remember a time in our lives when we shared one of our most cherished dreams for ourselves in leisure and were met with a long list of why that would be irresponsible, unaffordable, silly, embarrassing, unavailable, inaccessible, uninteresting and undoable. We have all had the spark of our passions put out by discouraging comments like these at one time or another.

For people who are devalued, these comments are all too common. For the sake of protecting people from all forms of social rejection or humiliation we try to distract them from their true wishes by starting with the reasons they shouldn't go after a certain passion.

This is especially true for those interests of which family members and support workers are ignorant. If we are not sure ourselves what resources exist out in the community to pursue a certain passion we tend to feel inadequate about providing intentional support to an individual.

Out of our own inadequacy, we unconsciously or consciously discourage another person's passion.

There are also times when we outright discourage another's passion because we do not personally like the activity or because we cannot envision ourselves supporting the individual to take part in a particular role. These prejudices must be confronted openly and directly. There is nothing wrong with feeling this way. What is wrong is letting our personal prejudices or lack of vision get in the way of exploring someone's passions and in providing them with support. As parents, friends and as support workers we must constantly be willing to admit when we feel discomfort with providing support ourselves and find another way for it to be provided.

For the reasons mentioned above, family members and support people may have the tendency to encourage those passions that require the least risk. This attitude of minimizing rather than managing the risk associated with pursuing new experiences is one of the main reasons why segregated programming has proliferated for so long.

Rather than discouraging others in their dreams we need to focus all of our energy on helping them make it happen. This focus must be on the concrete steps necessary for going after the passion. Firstly, exposing the individual to numerous opportunities for trying out the activity. Secondly, letting the person begin to define for themselves what aspect of the activity they most want to pursue. We also need to concentrate on finding others in the community that share the enthusiasm and passion and who can begin to assist the individual to establish themselves within that network.

5)   Developing Leisure Identities Involves a Strong Perception of Risk

Risk was a theme that emerged time and time again throughout the process. Some individuals were more willing to accept risks than others. For most, engaging in the dreaming/exploring process required the taking of several risks. It was risky to dream, to believe all over again that someone was listening and honouring what they were saying. It was risky to accept that "staff" might only be there initially and that in the long run further support would come from "others" in the agency or in the community who they didn't already know.

Taking lessons either alone or with others and having to learn a whole new set of competencies; the possibility that they might not be welcomed into a particular community club or association; trying an adventure activity that would challenge their physical endurance, going after something they'd always wanted to do and risking the possibility of failure and of disappointments; all called for maturity and courage.

The story below illustrates one woman's story of taking risks and overcoming fears.

> Sherry really enjoyed the dreaming sessions. They seemed to bring her memories of happier times. She began to be more animated when she talked about her childhood. Her dream was to take up horseback riding. For her, horseback riding represented a cherished memory of her childhood. She still remembered as a child the first time she got to ride the horse her father had brought home. She was a tiny child, much smaller than others her own age. She felt so powerful on that horse. So much in control. Her parents had been proud of her.
>
> When we first talked about what kind of horseback riding she would be interested in she had no idea. We discovered a trail riding place where you could go riding in a group with a guide. The first evening, Sherry was terrified. She had no idea what to expect. She contemplated getting back into the car and going home. The horses looked as big now as they had in her childhood. She wondered if she could stay on the horse or if she would be kicked off. During the first trail ride the guide asked permission to take the horses for a gallop. There came a resounding "no" from the back of the line. Sherry would have no part of galloping while on her horse named "Cher." At first whenever Sherry went on the trails she seemed to be given the most non-compliant horse: the horse that wanted to eat weeds on the side of the trail or change directions. After a few evenings of trail riding it became clear that the trail horses can sense when a rider is not going to exert power over them. It wasn't until she learned how to rein in the horse properly and persuasively, that Sherry noticed a change in the horse's willingness to comply with her wishes.
>
> It took several trips to the ranch before Sherry began to feel comfortable on the horse. Each night she went through that look of terror as she mounted a new horse. The terror would soon dissolve during the slow methodical plodding of the horses in single file at the beginning of the trail. By now, Sherry had become used to trotting on the horses and holding on for dear life. She had even galloped on a straight stretch of field. But she had done nothing to prepare herself for what was to come. One night, Sherry had a horse that was particularly frisky. It seemed to want to break the line and kept rushing ahead to nudge the horse in front. The guide took us slowly down a steep hill into a muddy stream and then directly up the bank of another steep hill on the other side. When Sherry's horse got midway down the first hill it began to

gallop and with the same momentum coursed its own path up the other hill. As Sherry got to the top of the hill her horse quickly fell into pace with the others as if nothing had happened. Sherry was beaming from ear to ear. Just like from out of a wild west movie, her horse had cut loose, and so had she.

6) Development of Each Person's Leisure Identity has its Own Natural Rhythm and Learning Curve

Leisure identities have rhythms of their own – rhythms that may be seasonal, or reflect the learning curve. Leisure identities that are seasonal usually require finding "off season" involvements. These may be such that they keep the flame alive and are in some way related. Fly Fishermen often spend their winters tying flies and preparing their equipment as they are anticipating spring and the opening of salmon fishing. Other off-season involvements may be intentionally quite different in order to give a contrast or break to the intense investments made during the "season."

In terms of the learning curve, some leisure involvements require a tremendous amount of investment initially to learn some of the basic skills, while others require only a small investment upfront and then a greater one, as the devotion and commitment to the activity grow.

Clearly, one of the most difficult and frustrating aspects of providing intentional support in the area of building leisure identities is the need to pay attention and recognize when enough is enough. Individuals need to be helped to indicate as much as possible when they want support and when they don't. There are times when even the keenest individuals need to take a break from their leisure and focus on other aspects of their lives.

Each leisure identity has its own natural rhythm. Part of the joy for the individual and the challenge for the support person or family member is in finding it.

7) People Tend to Learn Skills Related to Their Passions at a More Accelerated Rate Than Usual

People tend to learn skills related to their passions at a more accelerated rate than usual. This is not surprising. It is clearly much easier for all of us to learn skills and competencies when it is fun to learn and we get pleasure from doing it, when there are people with us who we enjoy and value, and when learning the skill is relevant and has a direct benefit to us. As individuals began to develop skills and competencies within their interest, they gradually began feeling more confident and more willing to take the required risks.

Learning a new skill may open doors for us. It may introduce us to new people, who share our passions, and it may allow us to explore other aspects of our chosen leisure identity.

There is also the aspect of role potency. A certain competency may really help in embedding the identity and strengthening the image we have of ourselves and the image others have of us. Learning to hit the ball in baseball really assists in building the identity of "baseball player" due to the importance this aspect of the role has for being seen as contributing to the team.

8) Providing Support to Maintain a Leisure Identity is as Important as Supporting its Development

A critical aspect of leisure identity development is in the area of maintenance. Individuals need support to remain engaged and involved in exploring a specific leisure identity. The single most detrimental barrier to this work is the unwillingness of individuals and/or agencies to commit energy and resources over time, to ensure that the person's leisure identities flourish and grow.

Too often, once these exciting initiatives are off the ground, the energy that was brought to bear in the beginning starts to dissolve. Community relationships that were fostered are left to maintain themselves. The constant vigilance and attention are no longer there. Family members and support workers lose interest. They are drawn elsewhere to lend a hand or they move on to another issue. The leisure aspect of the individual's life is expected to stay together without any additional support. This can be devastating to individuals with disabilities, who experience the withdrawal of support as another major discontinuity in their lives. It is clear from this project, that an ongoing commitment of support must be made to individuals who enter this process.

9) Relationships with Connectors and People Who are Part of the "Associational" Life of the Community Must be Fostered

Working within a human service setting can be a tremendously isolating experience. We often get so used to looking inward for resources that it becomes difficult to go outside into the community. From the beginning of the project, staff knew how essential it was that they look to the community for support and expertise. They began consciously seeking out community members very early in the process by inviting people to join the leisure committee who were integrally involved in community clubs and associations. (Kretzmann & McKnight, 1993) Leisure committee members were drawn from the community at large, the multicultural association, the arts community and the municipal recreation department.

Nine people from the community who had strong leisure identities and solid connections to their community joined the three-day leisure committee retreat. These people included a wine taster, birder, squash player, belly dancer, sculptor, billiards player, line dancer, quilter, and a tai chi student. Each of them told the story of how they got involved and what their participation has meant to them. They described their identities and gave committee members an opportunity to "try them out". Committee members saw clearly how leisure identities emerge naturally over time. Because they were part of the training, the nine individuals became familiar with the project goals and were able and willing to act as connectors for the project. As connectors, they offered to introduce those individuals who wanted to know more about their particular interest to others in the community that shared a similar interest.

From the outset of the project, staff had no idea if the individuals that we had introduced to the project would have the kinds of connections that would be helpful to the people included in the project. However, once individuals began unearthing their passions it became clear that it had been a worthwhile strategy . At least four of the individuals were drawn on to assist us in connecting some of the people we were supporting to others who shared their passion. They were also useful in teaching the support workers and the individuals about the resources available in the community.

In addition to the intentional strategy of searching out and nurturing these individuals before the project began, staff also fostered connections in the community as the need emerged, searching out people who shared the passion. Staff also found it useful at times to facilitate a connection between an individual and his instructor, if he or she had chosen to take lessons. Instructors tended to know who would be a good person to act as a bridger or connector to the other members of the club and/or associational community (Hutchison and McGill, 1992).

10) Overriding Concerns Must be Dealt With

For an individual to feel free to follow his passion(s) he must know that something is being done about one or two of the overriding concerns in his life. The story below is an illustration of how dealing with those concerns enabled an individual to be more content to develop his leisure interests.

Don wears army boots. In fact, he has a vast collection of army boots in his closet. He dreams about flying a jet fighter. He fantasizes about being in the military.

When we first asked Don about his dreams it was obvious that he wanted to be recognized as someone with courage and valour, some-one who helps others. He saw himself as someone who had gone up against all the odds and won. In fact he had. He had already survived 18 years of institutionalization and the abandonment by his family. This had shaped his perception of himself as a hero. However, his military image and dress had gotten him into no end of trouble since he moved out of the institution and into the community.

As leisure support workers we struggled with how to help him explore this fascination with war and the military without putting him into further jeopardy in terms of his image in the community. As we searched for the culturally acceptable outlets for these kinds of inter-ests we came across a variety of leisure identities including: being a member of the militia core; being a war game player; being an aviation fan; go-cart rider; and marksman.

Initially, we helped Don explore the possibilities of joining the army reserves in Brampton. He thought that being a member would give him an opportunity to hang out at the Legion and talk to other persons with the same interests. Through his early inquiries, Don was turned off by the extent that physical fitness and stamina were emphasized. He felt it was unlikely that he would be welcomed having a physical disability. Once he ruled out this avenue he began investigating the others.

We helped Don find out about a place that orchestrates civilian "war games" using guns with paint ball ammunition. This provided an oppor-tunity for Don to meet other men who enjoy dressing in army fatigues and boots and fantasizing that they are in "combat action." It was through participating in these games, that for the first time, Don seemed comfort-able reserving his army apparel solely for these kinds of settings.

The war games are physically rigorous. They require tremendous stam-ina and endurance. Don's difficulties with his balance made the games even more strenuous. For Don these games let him play out some of his fantasies. He was physically exhausted by them but exhilarated by the thrill of them.

After coming to know Don, it wasn't long before it was apparent that he had become obsessed with the tremendous amount of pain and pressure he felt in his head. He and his staff had spent a lot of time in the past 15 years going from doctor to doctor trying to determine the source of this pain. This was to no avail. The effect this had on Don was devastating. He had begun to see himself as a perpetual patient with no one to turn to for relief of the pain.

While we worked with Don on his leisure interests and began helping him focus on certain aspects of the identity, it was clear that he was distracted by his desire to find a way to control the pain he was experiencing in his head. In fact, he talked non-stop about it. We supported him to find a chiropractor who does cranio-sacral work. These alternative forms of treatment addressed Don's overriding concerns and made a real improvement in his ability to enjoy his life more and be fully present in his leisure involvements.

He chose throughout the project to focus on a cluster of activities that all seemed to have one thing in common, military adventure. While he was at the target range he was immersed in the moment without any thought about the pain in his head. When he put his helmet on and began racing around the go-cart course his expression was one of determination and courage. As he engaged in the fantasy world created by paint-ball enthusiasts, he had a concentration and willfulness that we had never before seen in him. When he was sitting beside the pilot in a small lightweight aircraft he was fully immersed in his long held fantasy that he was piloting a jet fighter.

One Final Word

If one desires a change,
one must be that change
before that change
can take place.

Gita Bellin

It is hoped that this resource book will be read and used by persons sincerely interested in bringing life back into our communities. Community is about being in relation to others and showing compassion to one another. Our passions are essential to community. Following our passions in leisure will help to bring a needed sense of balance to our lives that has been missing for so long. As each of us, including those of us with disabilities, reclaims those things in our lives that give us joy and a sense of zest for life, a new vital energy is created in our communities. Communities are re-energized when they consciously choose to take back into the fold those individuals who have been absent for so long, and who have been made to be reliant on human services. As clubs and organizations within the associational sector learn how to embrace and welcome home persons with disabilities they will take on new dimensions. With this, we are sure to witness a new vibrance and gentleness developing in ourselves and in our communities.

Selected Bibliography

Bellin, Gita. 1983. *A Sharing of Completion*. Los Angeles: Self Transformation Seminars.

Cheek, Neil. and W. Burch. 1976. *The Social Organization of Leisure in Human Society*. New York: Harper and Row, Publishers.

Cooley, Charles H. 1902. *Human Nature and the Social Order*. New York: Charles Scribner's Sons.

Dembe, Elaine. 1995. *Passionate Longevity: The Ten Secrets To Growing Younger*. Toronto. Macmillan Canada.

Gordon, C. Gaitz, and J. Scott. 1976. "Leisure and Lives: Personal Expressivity across the Life Span." In *Handbook of Aging and the Social Sciences*, eds. R. Binstock and E. Shanas. New York: Van Nostrand Reinhold Company.

Hayward, Susan. 1984. *A Guide for the Advanced Soul: A Book of Insight*. Avalon Australia: In-Tune Books.

Hutchison, Peggy, and J. McGill. 1992. *Leisure, Integration and Community*. Toronto: Leisurability Publications.

Kaplan, Max. 1979. *Leisure: Lifestyle and Lifespan: Perspectives for Gerontology*. Toronto: W. B. Saunders Company.

Kelly, John. 1987. *Freedom to Be: A New Sociology of Leisure*. New York: Macmillan Publishing Company.

Kretzmann, John, and J. McKnight. 1993. *Building Communities From the Inside Out: A Path Toward Finding and Mobilizing a Community's Assets*. Chicago Illinois: ACTA publications.

McCall, George, and J. Simmons. 1978. *Identities and Interactions*. New York: The Free Press.

Rajneesh, Bhagwan. 1983. *The Sacred Yes*. California: Rajneesh Foundation International.

Sheehy, Gail. 1995. *New Passages*. Toronto: Random House of Canada.

Stebbins, Robert. 1979. *Amateurs: On the Margin Between Work and Leisure*. Beverly Hills: Sage Publications, Inc.

Stone, Gregory. 1962. "Appearance and the Self." In *Human Behavior and Social Process,* ed. A. Rose. New York: Houghton Mifflin Company.

Wolfensberger, Wolf. 1983. "Social Role Valorization: A Proposed New Term for the Principle of Normalization." In *Mental Retardation,* 21(6), 235-239.

Wolfensberger, Wolf, and S. Thomas. 1983. *PASSING (Program Analysis of Service Systems' Implementation of Normalization Goals: Normalization Criteria and Ratings Manual.) (2nd ed.).* Toronto: National Institute on Mental Retardation.

About the Author

Judith McGill lives with her family in Waterdown, a small town near Hamilton, Ontario. She is an avid hiker, enjoys crafts and is now just beginning to explore the role of dancer. She is currently working to help create an intentional community in her area that will operate as a community supported agriculture (CSA) biodynamic organic farm.

Professionally, Judith has been training and consulting in the field of leisure integration for 14 years. She is co-author of *Leisure, Integration and Community*, with Peggy Hutchison and co-editor of *The Pursuit of Leisure: Enriching the Lives of People Who Have a Disability* with Deborah Gold. She has written numerous articles related to leisure integration, and was a board member and Editor of the *Journal of Leisurability* for ten years. She has a Masters in Environmental Studies from York University in Toronto, focussing on social policy.

Judith has extensive experience in advocacy work and for eight years was Senior Advisor to People First of Ontario, a self-advocacy movement of people labelled mentally handicapped.

Developing Leisure Identities: A Pilot Project has emerged from many years of workshops on the topic, as well as her involvement in the pilot project through Brampton Caledon Community Living.

She can be contacted to do training and consulting work at her address in Waterdown: P.O. Box 1265,
Waterdown, ON L0R 2H0
Canada
phone/fax (905)689-2891

or through

Brampton Caledon Community Living
34 Church St. W.,
Brampton, ON L6X 1H3
Canada
phone (905) 453-8841